SE

BREAKING NEGATIVE CYCLES

First published by Seth Whitted 2022

ISBN: 979-8-9872990-0-5

TABLE OF CONTENT

MY INSPIRATION

I'm, by far, the most extreme friend and relative when it comes to reaching my goals and my loved ones remind me of it often. Sometime I cut out all forms of entertainment for an extended period of time to focus on the business or I'll cutout bad foods to improve my health and more. Life is about balance, and I'm thankful God brought me balance in the form of a beautiful woman. I'm extremely thankful and appreciative to have you in my life, Cassie. God brought you into my life when I was at my lowest point, which was one of the reasons I didn't ask you out right away. I'm glad I swallowed my pride and took a chance. You've been my biggest accountability partner, friend, teacher, inspiration, and love of my life. You also brought me my little Story, who has both of our personalities. I'm thankful for both of you. Actually, I'm thankful for the three of you. I know Brixx is still cooking in your belly, and I can't wait to meet the prince.

Mom, I'm so proud of you. You've inspired me my entire life to want more and go after it with intensity. You've never let me believe that I was only capable of so much. You always told me you were proud, but that I could dig deeper. I wish you could see me grow, and I hope you're watching. The purpose of my journey is to bring you a better life and see you enjoy the fruits of your children. So, I want to dedicate this book to you. From that moment when I was young, the school and doctors said I would have to take medication for me to reach my full potential, you told me not to let anyone's opinions define me. You said I'd always have to work harder than everyone, and you charged me to do just that. I hope I haven't disappointed you because I stopped outworking everyone else. It wasn't enough; I had to start outworking myself. ***I owe everything to you, Ma Dukes. I love you.***

1

RULES SAVE YOU FROM YOUR EMOTIONS

"At the end of your feelings is nothing, but at the end of every principle is a promise." —Eric Thomas

Before we get started, I want to make a disclaimer. Although I offer guidance and advice throughout this book, I am in no way, shape, or form implying that any of it will be simple or easy to follow. I repeat, most of this advice will be a struggle to implement, but I challenge you to no longer look at struggle as a negative thing. Embrace it and choose to struggle toward what you want. Breaking negative cycle to change for the better was and still is a war for me, and this book will break down each of those changes. So, no, holding yourself accountable not be easy, but if you want to change your current circumstances, it's a must.

One of the best ways to make sense of difficult emotions is to write about them. According to Dr. Gail Matthews's study[1], writing down your goals makes you 42 percent more likely to accomplish them. Writing also improves your thought processes and critical thinking skills. So, as you read this book, I suggest you keep a notepad nearby or start a new note page on your phone or computer —whatever works best for you. Throughout this book, I will pose several questions for you to think and write about, and it's important for you to take some time to pause, reflect, and write a thoughtful response. This one simple task will be life-changing.

---

[1] Gail Matthews or Peter Economy, "This Is the Way You Need to Write Down Your Goals for Faster Success," *Inc.* https://www.inc.com/peter-economy/this-is-way-you-need-to-write-down-your-goals-for-faster-success.html.

DECISION-MAKING

Every day, each and every one of us makes decisions, and those decisions are like transactions you make at a store; you often get what you pay for. Take a few minutes now to write down some of the decisions, either big or small, that you've made so far this week. What did you decide to eat? Who did you spend most of your time interacting with? How did you spend the past twenty-four hours? What did you spend money on? Don't judge the reasons why you made those decisions right now; simply write them down.

Now that you have your list, go through each decision and ask yourself what you got or will get in return. Again, do not judge or try to justify the decisions; simply answer the question. For example, last week, I went to the gym four times, I ate a lot of fried foods, drank alcohol, and didn't sleep much so I could finish writing. As a result, my muscles feel tight, which is good, but I also feel bloated. I'm extremely tired from a combination of the lack of sleep, the workouts, and my terrible diet. Because of these decisions, I probably will not see any physical improvements, and I won't have enough energy to write any more chapters of my book.

Next, I want you to think about what you want out of life. What do you want to change about it? What brought you to this book? Take a look at your list of decisions again and next to each one, write down what you could have done differently to get what you really want. For example, I want to have as much energy as possible so I can be productive, and I want to improve my health and physique. So, to achieve that goal, I could limit my consumption of fried food and alcohol to special occasions, go to the gym at least two more days a week, and set a better schedule to ensure I get six to eight hours out of sleep.

Now, let me tell you what really happened last week. I went to the gym each of the first four days of the week. But on the fifth day, my wife, Cassie, got a call saying her father could pass away any day, so we drove to the hospital late at night to see him. He ended up passing away the next day, and I was there for her every minute. There wasn't much time to cook, so I ordered out the next few days. I also made sure Cassie had time to herself to grieve, so I cared for the baby while also handling business at work. These are all the excuses my mind will use to justify the decisions I made, but the results I want don't care about my circumstances. To be completely honest, I could have handled things ten times better, and I chose not to. I could've called my job, used paid time off, and told them I needed a few days to be with my wife. This would have helped me get more sleep and have time to plan out healthier meals. So, no matter what the circumstances were, I could've made better decisions to reach the goals I set for myself. This is why I said you should not try to justify your decisions because there's always a good reason to not remain disciplined.

Your decisions can be broken down into two categories: rule-based and emotion-based. By the end of this chapter, you will understand the importance of creating your own set of rules to ensure you make the change you want and effectively head toward the goals you want to achieve.

EMOTIONAL DECISIONS

Emotional decision-making refers to the choices you make based on how you feel. Are you upset? Tired? Sad? It could also be based on how your decision will make others feel. Will they be insecure or happy? Will they respect you more? For example, although I was never clinically diagnosed, I've always battled some form of depression. In those dark moments, I didn't feel like getting things done. The darkness

I felt said no to socializing and going after opportunities, and my negative mindset made me believe that things wouldn't work out in my favor.

By feeding into those dark moments, I felt even more like shit, which lead to more negative thoughts that made me feel like something was wrong with me. I often found myself praying and asking God, "Why is nothing working for me? Why can't I grow? Why are good things happening for everyone else but me?" It was as if the poor decisions I made were justified because of how I felt. I completely ignored the connection between my decisions, my mindset, how I felt, and my lack of success. To be honest, I was blinded by my talents. I had this belief that because I was extremely talented and grew up under poor life circumstances, I was somehow entitled to opportunities. I believed that someone would come find me, and that success was inevitable. I was in a never-ending emotional decision-making spiral.

I learned that, to succeed, I would have to change my entire outlook on life and the decisions I make. First, I had to understand that life does not care about where I came from or how talented I am. The only way I'll achieve success is through sweat equity, good decision-making, and hard work. Second, I realized I needed to change how I reacted to negative life situations, which is why I began developing rules and principles to make sure I always get the results I want, no matter what happens to me or around me and no matter how I feel. For instance, if I want to finish writing a ten-chapter book in thirty days and I set a goal to complete one chapter every three days, then no matter what happens, I need to make sure I get it done. I don't care if my house burns down or if my computer dies. I'll have to find a way to get that chapter done.

If you're not intentional with your decision-making,

your emotions will use any life emergencies or circumstances as an excuse to not execute on your goals, so you must set a rule. When you were a child, there was a rule to brush your teeth when you woke up. No matter what happened in your life, you found some time to brush your teeth. And that rule carried on into adulthood. Even if you are thirty minutes late for work, chances are you'll still brush your teeth because it's a rule you've set for yourself.

"Make decisions based on the outcomes you want, not your emotions." — Unknown

RULE DECISIONS

Rule decisions are based on the results and outcomes you want. "If I do this, then I'll get that," or "When this happens, I'll do this." To achieve a better outcome, you must establish rules for specific scenarios. For example, in those dark times I mentioned earlier, I made a rule to read and listen to inspirational books, meditate on the life I wanted, watch motivational and informative YouTube videos, or read the Bible for at least thirty minutes every day, no matter how I felt. Even if I didn't feel depressed that day, I still had to complete one of those tasks. I made a rule to unfollow anyone on social media who was negative, only get social media notifications from successful people I looked up to, and eat healthier. Sticking to these rules not only brought me out of these dark moments, but they brought me more information that helped me find my purpose, which, in turn, helped lessen the frequency of my dark moments. Later on, when I was brought back to my rock bottom, these rules came in handy (we'll talk a little more about this rock bottom in chapter 5). It's been years since I've dealt with any form of depression or dark moments, but I will follow these rules for the rest of my life. I learned that they were God's way of talking to me.

Making these rules and sticking to them was not, and still isn't, easy. It took a lot of trial and error to find what worked best for me. I just knew that the results I got from my emotional decisions never got me out of a dark space. Instead, they put me deeper into my depression and caused more problems. But the rules and principles I set for myself gave me definitive steps to follow and an opportunity to seek happiness and positive change.

I challenge you to start paying more attention to your decisions and the motivations behind them, especially after you've gone through hard times. Take notice of how you handled the moment. What happened as a result of your decisions, and how would you handle the situation differently next time? Once you've uncovered the answers for that specific situation, put a rule in place for yourself and find a way to practice following it. On a smaller scale, you can review the past twenty-four hours and analyze the decisions you made. This tactic can be used for many areas of life, including mental and emotional health, career, physical fitness, family, entertainment, and more. It can help to ask yourself what you want to accomplish and if the decisions you make will get you there. Start making a list of your principles and read them every day. Keep the list organized because, as life goes on, you'll continue to add to it.

Remember, most people who are in a negative cycle have no idea why, so keep an open mind, question everything, and don't look at anything as small or harmless. After all, it's the little things that add up to become something significant.

I once worked with someone who always experienced unfortunate events. Not one month went by without something bad happening to them, whether it was random health issues, car breakdowns, or a death in the family. So many things called for their attention that they didn't have any personal or sick time left because they had already used it up. Meanwhile, I had accumulated more than four hundred hours of sick time and sixty hours of personal time. Every time I spoke with this person, they complained about work, other staff members, or some aspect of life. I can't recall them ever saying one positive thing. I would constantly try to make this person see that their decision-making was purely emotional and negative. I would even tell them directly when I no longer had the patience to listen to their drama. They couldn't see that their mindset and decision-making were the reason for the endless cycle they were in. They didn't set any rules or principles to attract positive outcomes in their life. They seemed to be content with living in an endless cycle of reacting then complaining about the negative circumstance they were dealing with.

Imagine if they simply asked someone, "What is it about me that attracts all these negative events?" Someone could have easily opened their eyes. We all have things about us that we can't see. Make it a rule to periodically check in with yourself and discover your potential blind spots.

2

YOUR BLIND SPOTS CAN BE AN ASSET OR A LIABILITY

Blind spot (noun): the aspects of ourselves we aren't fully conscious of

Is there someone in your life who has potential but can't seem to get it together or accomplish anything? This could be a family member, a friend, a coworker, or anyone you spend considerable time with. You see exactly where they fall short and the connection between their decision-making and the circumstances they continuously deal with. You know deep down that if they just listened to you, they would be in a better place. But when you've attempted to help this person, they either couldn't hear you, became so prideful that they started an argument, or didn't care as much as you did. So, now you're left in a weird place where you constantly ask yourself if you should remain quiet, instigate an argument, or distance yourself from them because they disturb your peace. Does this sound familiar?

"People are quick to point out flaws in others but never quick to point out their own."— Unknown

Sorry to burst your bubble, but I guarantee there is someone in your life who feels this way about you on some level. Someone in your life can see things about you that stand in your way. They'll either bring it up to you all the time, remain quiet to avoid arguing, or wait for the right moment to have the conversation with you. Think about the last time you had to defend a decision you made or habit you have with someone who was close to you. These are usually tough conversations for us and our loved ones to have because, as humans, we tend to build up superior beliefs about ourselves that justify the bad decisions we make. The people who care about us just want to see us do better in life.

Little do we realize, these tough conversations can be an asset and the fastest route to overcoming the obstacles we've been struggling with and achieving our biggest goals. I realized this when I was just a teen. One time, I was playing with my little cousin Javon, who is about ten years younger than me. I realized then that if he could see what I saw, he would always be ten years ahead of his time. But how can you teach a four-year-old to see things like a fourteen-year-old? Even to this day, I tell him that listening to my generation is like having a time machine that goes ten years into the future. I have so much respect for my little cousin, and I'm proud of his willingness to listen and want to learn more. He has inspired me to be remain a student.

We all have traits and characteristics that stand between us and the things we want out of life; some are known, and others are not. Someone may continuously choose abusive partners, someone else may be talented but never accomplish anything, someone may be stuck in low-income housing, or someone could have untreated mental health issues. It's completely normal to have these problems. I assume that since you're reading this, you would like to improve upon or break out of your potentially bad habits. I encourage you to open your eyes to the things about yourself that you ignore.

Have you ever wondered why many accomplished individuals and experts always have a team around them? Have you ever wondered why smart people, like Mark

Zuckerberg, Elon Musk, Warren Buffett, Jay-Z, and Michael Jordan surround themselves with people who are smarter than them? Have you ever paid attention to how P. Diddy talks about working under LA Reid? Have you ever paid attention to how often successful people talk about their mentors and therapists? The brightest people in the world understand that a key ingredient to positive growth, success, innovation, and long-lasting success is surrounding yourself with people who not only point out your flaws but offer great insight and advice. So, if they're willing to invest in these tough conversations, why are we so quick to fight everyone and defend ourselves?

"There is a natural firmness in one's mind that won't be changed by trifle but, once unlocked, discovers a cabinet of fortitude."—*Thomas Paine*

WHY YOU CAN'T SEE YOUR BLIND SPOTS

There are many reasons why we might not be receptive to constructive criticism from others, but for now, I'm going to talk about five of the most common ones from my perspective.

First, we might not be mature enough. At every stage of life, we think we have things figured out and hold strong to those beliefs until a life-changing event occurs or someone we respect tells us something that changes our mind.

Second, our egos may be so large that we believe we're better off than we actually are. This thought may occur because people around us seem to be worse off than we are or because we pay more attention to the people who are suffering. It's easy to turn on a reality show, laugh at the dumb decisions others make, and feel good about ourselves because we don't seem to have as much drama as they do.

One year for Mother's Day, my siblings and I created a video for my mom. In it, we praised her for how she raised us. We talked about how we don't have kids out of wedlock running around, how we're not on drugs, how we're all hardworking, and how our success was due to her teachings. My mother responded to the video via text and said, "What makes you think you've made it? Because your lives aren't as bad as others? Your full potential has not been reached. Never feel that you have arrived. I'm proud of all your accomplishments, but there is more work to be done." At first, the response threw me off, but I realized she was making sure we don't use others' flaws to make ourselves feel better and that we stay focused on our long-term goals.

Third, we might not care. We may realize how much hard work is involved in changing, and we'd rather continue living life the way we have been.

Fourth, someone we respect in our life made similar decisions as us and lived in a similar way and, because we respect them so much, we believe this is the way we should keep living. As a kid who grew up in a single-parent home, I often observed my friends who had fathers present in the home. I noticed that a lot of their decision-making processes and mindsets came from them. This is something I run into all the time when I record my podcast with my cohost. There are some stances and mindsets they carry that I don't because I didn't grow up in a house with a male figure. Sometimes this is positive, and sometimes it's negative.

Fifth, traumatic experiences may make us pessimistic or narcissistic. We either see new information as negative or we don't trust the person it is coming from. This person could show they are trustworthy and honest for five-plus years, but the trauma runs so deep that we still can't see the positives or trust them enough to follow along and see where their advice leads.

HOW TO MAKE YOUR BLIND SPOT AN ASSET

Once you get out of your own way and are willing to listen to constructive criticism about your blind spots, you'll progress a lot faster in life. Something that might have taken you five years to change could take you a week. You might be asking, "How can I recognize what I can't see, and how do I become someone who can handle the truth?" There are a few things you can consider to get started.

First, do you actually want to change?

To get started, you actually have to have the desire and hunger to grow. Pray for God to open your eyes and show you how to get to the next level. Here's a mantra you can say daily with your prayers: "Lord, expand my mental and emotional capacity so I can see the things about myself that I currently can't. Expand my capacity to see my blind spots and hear what others have to say about them."

Second, ego is the enemy.

Remove your ego and understand that there is always more to learn. Michael Jordan is arguably the greatest basketball player to walk this earth, but every year he played, he grinded hard to be better. He even hired Tim Grover, a notable trainer and motivational speaker, to help take his skills to the next level. Imagine the greatest basketball player on Earth saying, "I need to get better. I'm weak in this area and need help."

Michael even said it himself in a Jordan commercial, "Maybe I led you to believe it was easy when it wasn't ... failure gave me strength. Maybe I led you to believe that basketball was a God-given gift and not something I worked for every single day of my life." Greatness comes when a person removes their ego and figures out how to get better, even when everything and everyone is already telling them they're great.

Third, read the signs.

Third, learn to read the signs. You will feel when your weaknesses are shown to you. As an example, have you ever been talking with a friend or coworker and they tell you your breath stinks? Instantly, you feel a tightness in your stomach. It's a combination of anger, embarrassment, or maybe anxiety. The reason you felt that way is because someone recognized something about you that you should've been able to see for yourself. Remember that feeling because it's an indicator that this may be an area of improvement. Instead of lashing out at your friend for trying to help you out, change how you react to that feeling. Ignore the emotions that come up and become curious. Ask yourself questions and seek answers. Investigate your friend's thought process. I guarantee they have been tiptoeing around this topic for a while, and the more they believe you can handle the truth, the more they will tell you everything they see. They're only going to go as far as your reactions let them unless they're someone who doesn't care about your feelings, like a parent, sibling, or spouse.

There are plenty of moments when my wife brings a weakness of mine up, and I instinctually want to fight back. Most times it's because she knows how to push my buttons! But one of my rules is to become curious about that instinct because it could be pointing to another area of improvement. Once I start asking questions, I learn a good lesson, and I can peacefully walk away with something to work on.

Fourth, create your board of experts.

Approach the people you respect and love and tell them that their honesty is important to you because your future depends on them keeping it real and pointing out the flaws and strengths you cannot see. Create an honest and growth-oriented community around you. The more you make honesty a priority in your circle, the faster everyone will grow. This has always been something my friends and I have been good at, and it's one of the reasons I feel we are all still close. When one person grows, the next person grows.

So, I challenge you to make a list of the people in your life and put them into categories based on what they are great at, whether it's finances, emotional maturity, relationships, mental health management, parenting, or their career. After checking in with them, tell them about the problems you're having or the goals you're trying to achieve in their particular area of expertise. Let them know that your success is dependent on their honest feedback. Most of them should take that responsibility seriously. It may be awkward at first, but once they cross that honesty threshold and see your positive reaction, they will continue to be an asset in your life.

3

FIRED BY GOD AND HIRED AGAIN

I've always had a hard time coming to terms with the idea that God is always watching. He knows what you are going to do before you do it. Similarly, statements like "Everything happens for a reason" or "I wouldn't change my past for nothing because it made me who I am" always made me curious. My discernment kicks in every time those lines come up in a conversation.

First, let me say that I was raised in the church, and I lived in the heart of the streets. I was also the child who questioned everything and needed things to make sense to go along with them. This curiosity has led me to seek answers from God on numerous occasions. The statements I previously mentioned have been passed down from generation to generation, and in my opinion, they are said to simply make the person feel better. These statements make you look at all of your mistakes, wrongdoings, or bad decisions, and say, "These things were supposed to happen so I could become the man or woman I am today." But let's break this down.

Let me be clear: I don't believe God is limited in any capacity. I also don't believe He's sitting around watching all of us at every second, and I don't believe He designed a world He can control like a game of Grand Theft Auto. I believe He designed a world that gives us control, free will, and the ability to access His power through faith.

I'll prove it. In Genesis, God didn't know that Adam ate the apple until He found him hiding, ashamed of his nakedness. God knew that if Adam was able to feel fear, shame, and guilt, he must've eaten the forbidden fruit.

Before eating the apple, man didn't know fear, hate, doubt, or any other evil that distracts you from your calling and purpose. A life not focused on purpose is death, and this is the battle we face with our flesh. This is what was meant by "You will die if you eat the fruit." It wasn't about dying and leaving this world in a coffin. It was about having all of these mental and emotional barriers that stand between you and your purpose. Man was able to only see good, and now, man can see and feel evil. With good, all things are possible, there are no limitations or lack, and life is fruitful. But evil is the part of us that is fearful, hateful, jealous, insecure, doubtful, shameful, or addicted. So, in the story of the Garden of Eden, God did not know Adam ate the apple, nor did He know beforehand that Adam would disobey. I'm sure He knew it was possible for a human to disobey Him, but according to scripture, once He saw the disobedience, He issued more consequences to them. If God is always watching, then how did He not know of Adam and Eve's decisions?

The statement "Everything happens for a reason" really turns my discerning eye on as well because I know people who will not initiate any positive life moves because of this mantra. They believe things will fall into place because God has a purpose for them. In my opinion, God doesn't have a specific plan or purpose laid out for every single person. I believe that 1) God has His own purpose and missions, and we may have the opportunity to carry one out on His behalf; 2) He can, will, and does use every positive and negative situation for His purpose; and 3) God calls specific people at specific times for a certain purpose. I just don't believe this is done for everyone and every situation.

So, I guess the statement is true; it's just that some people may be looking at it incorrectly. Some things happen by chance, some things are meant to be, and some things happen as a result of someone's decisions. In my opinion, God sent His only son not only as a sacrifice but as a living example of what we could accomplish while battling this flesh. We have to stop undermining Jesus's accomplishments on this earth. The one we call Jesus was not superhuman the way we're taught. He faced the same fears and doubts as us, but he succeeded at finding the kingdom within. He rose to the occasion, controlled his instinct to judge, and was able to achieve ultimate self-mastery. He was able to achieve the lifestyle and mindsets that man experienced before eating the forbidden fruit. According to the books written by his followers, it took him close to thirty years to master the ability to use faith in a miraculous way. So according to my theory, Jesus had a mission, but it wasn't guaranteed that he would succeed. He was human just like us. He even showed us his doubt and fear when he wept and asked God to take the task from him. But he got it together and moved forward. He could've easily made different decisions. I've never heard a Christian voice this idea, and it's sad because you miss out on some very important lessons when you simply look at Jesus as God personified. We undermine what he accomplished by not understanding that he was born in flesh, mastered the flesh, and challenged us to do more than he did.

I say all of that to say every one of us at every moment has the ability to achieve success or find a purpose that God can use us for. For me, it's easier to stay on track when I'm mentally, emotionally, and spiritually where God needs me to be. I can't speak for other people, but God has shown me this for myself. Maybe it's the same for you. All of the years I spent not being where I'm supposed to be, i call dead time that I can't get back. Some people would say those moments made me who I am, and while that's true, I know I missed out on a lot of opportunities during those times. If you're reading this book, you're most likely in the same boat as me. Be honest with yourself and realize that you may have missed out on opportunities. Don't try to make yourself feel better by thinking your misfortune was all by design. But also know that your life isn't over. Now that you've gone through that and learned the lesson, the key is to never make those same mistakes again.

I call the years between ages twelve and twenty-seven my "dead time." If you're not a spiritual person, you might not be able to understand where I'm coming from, but I'm not saying that those moments didn't make me who I am. I'm not saying I didn't enjoy the good times I experienced or learn from the bad times. What I'm saying is, as far as following my purpose goes, that was my dead time. I wasn't walking the path God had for me; it was like I was running on a treadmill for years until I got off and got in the real race.

STRIKE 1

The core reason I "missed the boat" several times is because I was a people pleaser and had a deep-rooted need for external validation. As I write this book, I'm realizing that my need to feel validated by others was disguised as marketing and branding. I thought I was being strategic, but I was actually feeding a deep insecurity.

The real race involves being authentically yourself, knowing what your mission is, and going after it day after day. When I was young and in the midst of my dead time, God revealed to me that my purpose was in content creation. Although I was extremely productive with making music and generating money from other business ventures during those years, I didn't get any further than where I was. I was chasing a lifestyle and making art a specific type of way, completely ignoring key elements that I believe God was looking to use. And again, I believe if you're not trying to fulfill your purpose, you're just running in place on a treadmill until God knocks you down or you realize what you're supposed to be doing. I also believe that if you don't figure it out quickly, you'll miss your current purpose. And the wildest part is when you miss your purpose, you'll feel it. You will most likely deny it like I did. This was the delusional thought process that kept me away from my purpose.

I believe God had a mission and purpose for me in the music industry, and in 2014, it hit me that I had missed the boat. Strangely enough, I realized I missed it before then as well. There are plenty of purposes God offers people, and it is our job to figure out the current one. So if you missed a purpose, learn from it and get ready so you don't miss the next wave. God doesn't care if it's you or Jeff who lives down the street; He will find someone to complete His mission.

My need for validation combined with my drive to get out of poverty, help others, build my community, succeed at music, and help my struggling mother led me to a lifestyle of making things happen by any means necessary. I sold drugs and cars, robbed people, financially used women, gambled, bought and flipped cheap items on eBay and Craigslist, worked a full-time job, coached kids, promoted and hosted parties, shot photography and music videos, ran a photo booth business, sold mixtapes, and attempted many other hustles that I've now forgotten about. I had a plan to generate enough money to fund the music. Needless to say, you can't get good things with evil. None of my money moves were about greed. I was just a young man who lacked the wisdom and guidance to know that you can't build anything indirectly. I also learned that you can't use evil methods. You have to sacrifice for what you want or nothing will ever get built.

STRIKE 2

Another aspect I fell short in was the brand, style, and market I focused on. Since I came from a high-crime environment where everyone around me, including myself, was selling drugs and hustling, this was the market I put my focus into. Although I was filled with knowledge, spiritual insight, and energy, I kept myself in a box because I wanted the love and validation of my peers. No disrespect to Common, Talib, and similar artists, but I didn't want to be anything like them. My friends and I were big fans of Jeezy, G-Unit, Jay-Z, and Yo Gotti, so I put more energy into making music for that crowd. I didn't realize that if I was 100 percent myself, I could've created a whole new wave that would've brought multiple crowds together. The hood and my bros used to always say, "Chill on that conscious shit. Don't nobody wanna hear all that."

Don't get me wrong. My music was all me; there were no lies. I just ignored an entire side of myself to win over the street crowd. I've always been that way, probably from a combination of growing up in the church and in my particular neighborhood. I've always looked at church folks as corny, and I never wanted to be looked at in that way. Although I respect the majority of the people at church and I appreciate all of the love, I never wanted to be so disconnected from the world in the way they were. I noticed that many of the folks in church had no way of actually making a change in the community. Part of me didn't care how anyone felt about me, but there was also a small part of me I kept hidden because I knew I would get put into a box that would instantly disconnect me from the world. I should've recognized then that God had given me the gift of innovation.

In 2005, it hit me that I missed an opportunity when I was riding to work with a friend and he turned on a new artist who was just like me but without the gritty side. His name was Kanye West, and he completely changed the game.

The wildest part that always leaves me feeling a little bitter is that the same people I sought validation from would say, "You gotta get poppin' in your hood first. Don't nobody wanna hear that conscious music or that singing shit." Those people never gave me the validation I was seeking because I wasn't being 100 percent myself, and they typically did not hesitate to show their respect for those who were 100 percent themselves. These are the same people who would present me with artists who were similar to me and talk highly about them, saying stuff, like "Bro, I respect him because he wasn't afraid to take a leap of faith" or "He's fire and he's conscious like you, Murd" or "Yo, Murd, this dude be singing like you, and it's fire."

This is a common occurrence for people pleasers and validation-seeking folks. Most of us end up resenting the people around us for this, but I believe the fault and responsibility is on us. We have to be willing to walk alone. You can't expect to be different and fit in at the same time.

"No man can serve two masters."
(Matthew 6:24, KJV)

I paid the price for trying to be different and fit in by giving back to my community at the same time I was poisoning it for profit, climbing the corporate ladder and playing the streets at the same time, being an inspiring person and sleeping around with women I had no intentions of committing to long term.

Now, most likely, your out-of-control life circumstances have led you to possess a similar personality trait. The lack of balance and structure you miss out on from growing up in a single-parent home often leads to this type of insecurity. I understand how we all got here, but as humans, we have the ability to change and grow, so there are no excuses, especially if you're on a journey to succeed at something. Every road to success requires study. You must study yourself and your current habits and how those you emulate have succeeded. The road to success is largely a road of constant self-improvement, and I guarantee that while on that road, you will read something or hear someone talk about the detriments of people pleasing and seeking outside validation. You have to be ready to hear the hard truth. This won't easy, but it is a must if you're going to break the cycle you're in and achieve your goals.

Learning about and understanding your weaknesses is not supposed to start a pity party where you come up with excuses for why you're not succeeding. To me, it was liberating because I was determined to never let an opportunity pass me up again. So, if you are on the journey toward your purpose and you don't want to pass it up, keep reading. On the path toward your purpose, you must trust your gut, even if that means you walk alone or are uncomfortable or broke. We can't serve two masters at once. There is no cutting corners. Every other path, except the one leading to your purpose, will keep you running in place.

4

HIDDEN SINS

The topic of this chapter is a subject that is looked over far too often, so I wanted to give it proper attention. In my opinion, there is one powerful word people tend to consistently misunderstand and misuse: sin.

"Jesus answered them, 'Most assuredly, I say to you, whoever commits sin is a slave of sin.'"
(John 8:34, NKJV)

"But each person is tempted when he is lured and enticed by his own desire. Then desire when it has conceived gives birth to sin, and sin when it is fully grown brings forth death."
(James 1:14–15, ESV)

I believe we've all been taught to look at sin through the lenses of the church and the people who influence society and popular culture. The concept of sin has always been mind-twisting to me because its interpretation is based on the perception, desires, and emotions of the person who is using the term. For example, a pastor could preach a sermon about how living with someone before marriage or using drugs and alcohol is a sin while ignoring that he's overweight, addicted to food, and smokes cigarettes. The average reaction I get from this example is that I can't compare drugs and alcohol to food, but I strongly disagree.

As a child, I wanted to understand the true concept of sin. One day, God revealed to me that sin is less about right and wrong and more about missing the mark and being distracted from your mission. Anything that takes you away from your purpose causes you to sin and miss opportunities. For example, it is my opinion that smoking and drinking alcohol aren't sins in and of themselves. What makes these actions a sin is when they control you. If these actions keep you from doing God's work and you find yourself becoming less productive and putting it over doing good, you have entered the area of sin. If it forces you to miss the mark, then you are living in sin. This probably goes against everything most people are taught because the common notion is that sin is about the obvious feelings of shame that come with breaking the law or some other action that society deems wrong. You often feel shame after having sex with someone you shouldn't have, waking up hung over on Sunday morning, or robbing someone. But you don't necessarily feel shame after watching ten straight hours of Netflix, constantly spending on Amazon, eating fast food after the doctor told you you're prediabetic, or any other vice. Not to mention, most people, especially religious people, cherry-pick scriptures to make others look like wrongdoers while ignoring the scriptures that point the finger at their addictions and demons. I heard someone say once that you can't use the book of Leviticus to talk bad about homosexuality, then ignore when it talks about eat shrimp, pork, catfish, lobster, and every other "unclean," popular food.

This is why this topic closely connects to the last chapter; my lifestyle and actions caused me to miss the mark and be distracted from my mission. They led me away from where I needed to be to fulfill my purpose. I was living in sin. When Scripture says you will be a slave to the things you are addicted to, that doesn't just refer to drugs and alcohol; you could be addicted to TV and you'd be living in sin. But to the average person, it's just TV. The act of watching it is not wrong or outwardly harmful, so it's not a sin. This is how we've been taught, especially in America. We're taught that sin is what's perceived as wrong, but that is far from the truth.

In an effort to paint a clear picture for you, I want to be completely transparent. Here are some of the sins I had to overcome to stay focused on my mission: chasing money; using women for sexual pleasure; watching porn; masturbating; overconsuming alcohol, entertainment, and food; and people pleasing. Would you believe me if I told you pleasing people was my biggest sin? You'd probably guess that alcohol or chasing money and sex would be the biggest offenders, but my people pleasing habits were disguised as attributes of a good person. I had a deep-rooted belief that I had to put others before myself, take responsibility for how others felt, and never say no to helping someone, even if it meant saying no to what I wanted.

Once people can get away from the idea that sin is about being right or wrong and feeling shame, they can begin to unlock the power God has given them and walk in their purpose because they'll have the capacity to sit with themselves and figure out what their purpose is and what's keeping them from it. You must be honest with yourself if you're going to remove sinful blockages from your life.

Now, let's figure out what's causing you to miss the mark and stay distracted from your mission. Take a moment to think about the things, people, and events in your life that have caused you to be less productive and not walk in your purpose. What people, things, or actions no longer serve you in a positive way? Do these things consume you? Don't judge yourself for whatever comes up. Be honest and know that you are taking the first step toward fulfilling your purpose.

If you find that your blockages control you, don't feel forced to cut them out immediately; you don't have to stop enjoying yourself. You do, however, need to find a way to make sure they no longer control you. I still have a drink every now and then because alcohol doesn't control me in that way. Now, if you are someone who is negatively affected by alcohol, then it might be time for you to hang it up because it's causing you to miss the mark.

To successfully get back on track, you need to be able to recognize your shortcomings and blockages. So, if you haven't already done so, put this book down and dig deep to uncover what's causing you to miss the mark.

5

KARMA AND CONSEQUENCES

"In all my years as a clinical psychologist, I have never seen anyone get away with anything. I've seen people twist reality successfully because it doesn't snap back at them in the moment, but two years later, they get hit hard by something. They think it's unfair until we trace it back to them twisting reality."— Dr. Jordan Peterson

Every decision produces an outcome. No matter what your intentions are, there will be an outcome, whether it's positive, negative, or both. In my opinion, there are four types of outcomes: 1) an immediate outcome, 2) one that affects your reputation, 3) one that affects others around you, whether they are close to you or not, and 4) an unexpected outcome. In the streets, we call that last one a "humbug." Again, these outcomes can be positive, negative, or both. Let's discuss the negative side first.

Jim is a farmer in Kentucky. Every year, his organic farming process produces decent results. One spring, a farmer friend of his approached him with the idea to use a new chemical that sped up the growing process and produced bigger crops. Who wouldn't want to increase their productivity and the size of their product? After doing his research, Jim saw mixed reviews from both farmers and environmentalists, with many of them recommending people to stay away from the chemical because there was a chance it could cause issues. Jim also read reviews that said the chemical had worked wonders, and consumers seemed to enjoy the products as well. He decided to be positive and optimistic and move forward because the benefits could be life-changing.

Usually Jim's crops took about ninety days to

harvest, but with the new chemical, he could make it happen in just seventy. Before long, he harvested the product and got ready to deliver to the stores he had contracts with. The distributors asked Jim how his products were done so soon and why they were so big. When he told them about the new process he was using, they refused to accept his crops because of the uncertainty surrounding the chemicals. After all, they had previously signed agreements with their corporate customers that said the produce they supplied would be free of adulterants of any kind. They also reminded Jim that, according to the contract they signed with him, they were able to deny his products if they felt it would be harmful to their business. They told him to contact them when he returned to his organic process.

To make up for the lost income, Jim decided to sell what he had at the weekly flea market. He managed to sell a good portion of his harvest, which covered some of his expenses, but not as much as if he had sold it to the distributors. A week later, several people in town came down with unexplained health issues, reporting skin rashes, headaches, diarrhea, and flu-like symptoms. Health officials interviewed the patients, and when it was concluded that the individuals became sick after eating Jim's chemical-laden products, they speculated that was the cause. Environmentalists and local politicians used the media to caution others against purchasing products from farmers who used the chemical until they could conclude whether or not it was the cause of the townspeople's unexplained health issues. A full investigation to prove that the illnesses were caused by the chemicals Jim and other farmers used, but all signs pointed to the contaminated produce.

Recognizing his fault, Jim decided to issue a public apology and let people know that he would no longer use the chemical moving forward. He also spoke with his lawyer about settlements for those affected. He disposed of the remaining product and planted a new set of crops in a different area using his old organic process.

Let's talk about the consequences of Jim's decision to use chemicals and what outcome category they fit into. First, the immediate consequence was that the distributors turned Jim's business away, which affected both parties' income and caused them to find different ways to generate money. Second, Jim's reputation was now in jeopardy. Even though he corrected the issue, the distributors might decide not to carry Jim's product in the future because his reputation had been tainted. This one decision could cripple his farm for generations. Third, the customers' health was affected, not to mention the family members and friends who might've grabbed a batch to eat. Fourth, the humbug or unexpected consequence could be that the next crop season is a drought, equipment breaks down, or someone who typically helps with the farming becomes sick. Any of these events would cause further issues with Jim's farm and finances.

No matter who you are or who you become, you'll likely have to deal with one or more of these consequences. In my opinion, the key to lasting success is taking your consequences on the chin and developing an intense focus at the same time. Lawyers may disagree with me, but Jim made a great decision in owning up to his actions. The best thing we all can do is accept the lesson and plant the next set of seeds for the future harvest while maturely dealing with the current consequences. This is the hardest thing for people to do. It's hard to focus, plan, and execute on anything when you're dealing with the stress that comes with rough times. This is why many criminals are repeat offenders, why people who stop selling drugs end up starting again, why rappers who lose a rap battle fall off, or why some business moguls don't recover from bad press. The time right after the storm requires an understanding that you have some hell to pay while you plant new seeds for the future. Look at the difference between Ja Rule and Rick Ross after 50 Cent went after both of them. The "Officer Ricky" moment was supposed to bury Ross, but his resilience and work ethic made us respect him even more after.

I'm one of the many young men who lived with a "get it by any means" mindset for years. I truly believed that a combination of gambling, selling drugs, using people, working a full-time job, volunteering, making music, and filming would somehow get me where I wanted to be. I was so ambitious and motivated to change my family's negative circumstances that I pushed myself in every aspect of life, whether it was negative or positive. It hurts to look back at my younger self and the destructive mindsets I had, especially because I know there are other young men out there who want to change their circumstances but lack exposure and wisdom, just as I did.

I never wanted the bullshit that came with the street life. I wanted to avoid the attention, reputation, violence, jail time, and jealousy. I just wanted to use the money to kick-start my music career. But as you guessed it, things never worked out that way. In a way, I was just like Jim the farmer. Deep down, I knew I shouldn't have ignored the negative signs that have kept me away from the streets for so long. They were right in my face. Flex was on house arrest, Jonesy did time in jail, BT was always in and out of prison, Mob caught a gun charge, the majority of the old heads were doing Fed bids, and Paul and Matt both got murdered. Not one dude I know from the streets has successfully transitioned from that life to legitimate success and security. I also knew that God wanted me to put more faith into my mission instead of stressing over money. It's hard to not focus on where the money will come from, especially when you're young and dumb. But I now understand that when God has plans for you, you have to ensure you're making the correct moves. You don't ever want to work against the mission.

For example, God gave Moses specific instructions for approaching the pharaoh. Imagine if Moses, hearing these instructions, became impatient and decided to hire a hitman to kill the pharaoh instead. That would've gone against the mission. God wanted everyone to see him spar with the king of Egypt. He wanted the Earth to know who the God of all gods was and is. In my case, God wanted the glory. God wanted me to put my faith in his ability to provide so I could explain how things worked out for me, so I could realize it was all God. I wasn't supposed to take a comfortable route.

MY LAST ROCK BOTTOM

Using crime to generate money not only caused me to fail

my mission, but it also resulted in me having hell to pay. In 2014, God brought me back to rock bottom, the lowest point in my life. Everything hit me hard at the same time. This was God's way of showing me that I was on the wrong path. I was fed up. It felt like my hard work was always met with setbacks. All of the cars I invested in had broken down, I was robbed, I lost my job, and all the business credit cards I used to purchase equipment were in collections. My mother was kicked out of her home, and I had no way to help her out. And my sister was struggling in graduate school, but I couldn't help her either. I was a twenty-seven-year-old loser who had all of this deep knowledge but nothing to show for it. I was the best artist no one knew about. I felt useless every now and then, but for the most part, I still chose to see the positive in everything. I had dark moments that were followed by me snapping out of it and remembering my list of principles and rules. I had a deep understanding that I had hell to pay like Jim, but it was temporary. It still ate me up that I'd had it all wrong and others around me suffered because of it.

I remember driving to work in my Buick with its blown head gasket during the coldest winter ever. I had bought a bottle of antifreeze and three jugs of water and had to pull over every five minutes on I-376 to pour more antifreeze into the coolant overflow. I couldn't turn the heat on or the car would overheat. Also, my cell phone had broken, so I was temporarily using a flip phone. Through all of this, I still was able to battle the darkness that attempted to keep me in a rut. I would cry then laugh in the next breath because I would remind myself that it was all temporary. No one knew what I was going through, mainly because I was the one who was always there for everyone else. I had to keep it together.

ANGRY FAITH WORKS

In late 2015, while still in the midst of my rock bottom, I kept coming across the concept of faith. I'm extremely intuitive, and at that point of my life, I was extremely obedient. I began diligently studying faith with an open mind and God's guidance. He pointed out every scripture on faith, showed me YouTubers who discussed the topic, and even shared the documentary The Secret.

My studying went on for months without any significant breakthroughs. But then, I finally had one that changed everything for me. I hope you can open your mind and understand. As I shared earlier, I experienced an extremely low and dark moment of frustration. One day during that time, I was driving in my cold car. I had just left the gas station, where I had over drafted my bank account to fill up my tank, and found myself having to pull over yet again because the car kept overheating. I parked on the side of the road in the middle of the winter to give the car a few minutes to cool down. I had absolutely no positivity left in me, and I felt every emotion at once. I took all my anger out on God, screaming and yelling directly at Him. In my mind, I was learning and applying faith, but I hadn't seen any results. What's the point of studying something that isn't working? I thought. Growing up, I was taught that type of frustration was considered blasphemous in the organized religion world, but at that point, I didn't care. I remember being so pissed that I said out loud, "Where you at, Lord?! You see me grinding; you see us struggling, so where you at? All this faith, faith, faith; show me something!" If you truly understand faith and the teachings of the Son of God, you'll understand my frustration. It seemed to only work for small things, like finding a close parking spot, or it manifested as something I wasn't exactly applying my faith to.

At that time, money was on my mind. I felt

pressured to make a car payment ASAP because I was two months behind and my car was at risk of getting repossessed. To make matters worse, my mom needed financial help because the gas in her house was cut off in the middle of winter, and my wife and I were looking to buy a home, so I needed my portion of the down payment. My wife also wanted to go on a trip to visit her friend for New Year's, and it was expected that I pay. Plus, I wanted to make a music video that was projected to cost at least $5,000. My wife, Cassie, had no idea how bad my finances were.

"Therefore I tell you, whatever you ask for in prayer, believe that you have received it and it will be yours."
(Mark 11:24, ESV)

Out of anger and frustration, I began reminding God of His Word and promises. I attempted to hold Him accountable by explaining exactly what I expected from Him.

"Bet!" I said. "If you want me to have faith, show me something. Here's a car payment, a trip, a video project, heat for the house, and my purpose! Deliver those things, and I'll never sell drugs again and I'll dedicate myself to the purpose you have for me and apply faith. If you want me to have faith, then show me something!"

I was so fed up that I became reckless, delusional, and unreasonable. I really put God to the test. I called the company who financed my car loan and gave them my debit card number knowing I didn't have the money. I told Cassie to book the trip, and I called the videographer who quoted me for the music video and set a date to start filming. He told me he needed a deposit within the next week, and I simply said, "No problem, how much?" Every part of me was showing God that these things were now on Him to take care of. I was frustrated and had nothing to lose. I even told Cassie I would have my portion of the down payment. As reckless as it sounds, I said yes to everything I wanted knowing I was in the red.

A few days later, my supervisor called and asked if I could stand in her place at a meeting she couldn't make. When I arrived, my other supervisor, Candy, was there. After the meeting, Candy pulled me into the hallway and handed me an envelope. She said the company wanted to thank all the employees for our hard work with a holiday bonus. I walked back to my car with a huge grin on my face, talking to God.

"Hmm . . . let me find out you're trying to show me something," I said out loud. "Big Homie, you're wild if you did what I think you did. I'm not going to open it until I get to the car."

When I got in my car and opened the envelope, I

started laughing . . . hard. It was the kind of laugh where you can't breathe and tears are coming down your face. A $1,800 check was sitting in my lap. I felt like God was right next to me, laughing and saying, "You thought I was sweet, Lil Bro? Like this was too big for me? This is what I was trying to show you all along, dummy. You have to keep that same energy, but next time, watch your tone before I show you the other side."

At that moment, I got a glimpse of exactly how God operates. I spoke to Him and said, "You brought me to that level of frustration just to get me here, for me to see this?" The check was enough to cover my car payment, Cassie's New Year's trip, the down payment for the music video, and more. My brother had enough to pay my mom's gas bill so I didn't have to, but I still gave her some of the money. And the mortgage company came back and said they no longer needed the rest of the down payment. The icing on the cake?

Later that week, God showed me that He wanted me to provide content to the world and teach His principles through entertainment. Sometimes I believe my faith is the reason the entire company received a holiday bonus that year, but in all actuality the company changed from for profit to a nonprofit and decided to give employees bonuses to get rid of the surplus. From that moment on, everything I moved forward with out of faith worked out.

Before I get back to karma and consequences, let me attempt to explain all the factors that went into that moment of faith because every step is important. First, I made a firm decision about what I wanted to happen. The gift of faith is perfect and is based on us. If you're not sure what you want, then faith can't be applied. So being clear on what you want or need is the first step. Next, I reminded God of His promises and boldly stated what I needed. My entire life, I was taught that our God was stingy and that we would see the riches of life when we got to heaven. But the scriptures on faith revealed to me that God wants us to live prosperously here and now. We must meditate on faith and remind God of His promises. Then, I moved forward as if everything was taken care of. We activate faith when we move forward without doubt. Yes, I'm telling you to be bold and maybe even ridiculous. Remember, God's son fed thousands with a few loaves of bread and a few fish. Move forward with the plans that are revealed to you. Do what you can, and put the rest in God's hands. Finally, I envisioned what my desired outcomes would feel and look like. I had nonstop conversations about the video shoot, and I imagined what it would feel like to be on set. I just knew it would feel amazing to pay my car payment. Putting yourself in your future self's shoes is a powerful ingredient for faith. Remember that Jesus always asked, "Do you believe you are healed?" He needed the person to feel healed on a subconscious level as well.

My new understanding of how faith works was groundbreaking because I was at the point most people reach right before they turn back to the decisions that got them in a hole in the first place. A man newly released from prison might reach the point I was at and go back to selling drugs. The person who just got out of an abusive relationship might feel uncomfortable or lonely and go back to their partner. You have to be aware of this part of the process to break the cycle. I'd been there too many times, and I wanted to make sure that was the last time, so I had to commit to making a different decision. I knew it would be a rocky journey because I still had consequences to deal with from my previous decisions, but I was ready. It doesn't matter that you turned everything around; the real test comes from serving your sentence while having faith in the new seeds you're planting.

The five years following this showing of faith were still hell as far as my career and finances were concerned. No one around me knows this, not even my wife. Part of me is convinced that not speaking about my hardships to my loved ones is part of faith, but there's also a part of me that believes there's some deep-rooted pride in keeping it a secret. I can admit that I most likely have some trauma surrounding my issues. This may be a blind spot of mine, but I'll get back to that when I finally get answers.

After my breakthrough, I was completely locked in on playing offense, planting seeds in the now, and applying faith so the good outcomes could surpass the bad. I knew it would be a tough journey because I was starting over and had low income, but I told myself that the faster I served my sentence, figured out what my next steps were, and applied faith and work, the faster I could develop a process to learn these big lessons without going through that kind of storm ever again. I had a bright idea that if I searched for the lessons instead of letting life teach me, I could avoid the drama, and boy, was I correct. It's possible to receive the benefits of bumping your head without having to actually bump your head. Chapter 11 will break this process down in more detail.

To recap, recovering from the storm is a critical part of your journey. It requires awareness, understanding, and resilience. This is the part where people often say, "I tried to be better, but the streets kept calling me back." The key is to remember why you can't keep making those same decisions. You don't want to plant any seeds that will create more consequences than benefits and keep you in the dark longer. This recovery period is also a time when you can learn the most about yourself and figure out the areas you need to improve on. Last, you must surround yourself with positive information every day. Read or listen to books about accomplished people who can inspire you and teach you the skills and habits you'd like to develop. You can utilize Tik Tok, Instagram, Google, and YouTube for this as well, but be sure to check multiple sources to avoid running with misinformation.

JOURNAL ACTIVITY

Before we move on, let's take a moment to reflect and write a list. You can call it the "I'm not going back" list. On a sheet of paper or in your digital journal, write down all the reasons you want to break a particular habit or cycle. Write down all the direct and indirect consequences that come from engaging in this habit. Next, write down what causes you to perpetuate that cycle. What draws you to that situation? This list will not only be your reminder for why you're not going back, but it will also show you the information you should surround yourself with. The habits and cycles you struggle with have been overcome by others. There are countless books, podcasts, and vlogs you can look into to see what worked for them.

For example, one of my biggest downfalls is doing too many things at once and not being able to say no. At one point, I was working, coaching, selling dope, rapping, taking photos, shooting music videos, gambling, and saying yes to everyone with a good idea. On my list, I wrote down that I no longer wanted to spread myself thin. I didn't want to give my time and energy to anyone or anything that was outside of my purpose, and I wanted to narrow my focus and attention just one or two projects. I took those sentences, turned them into questions on Google and YouTube, and found books that changed my life. Good to Great by Jim Collins talks about the power of focusing on your strengths and saying no to everything else. Not Nice by Dr. Aziz Gazipura taught me how to say no, put myself first, and put an end to people pleasing and feeling responsible for others. Once you find books you like, take note of the resources those authors mention and why. Don't just read to read. Be intentional about progressing.

6

PERSONAL IMPROVEMENT PLAYBOOK

"In life, we're either progressing or slowly falling off. There's no way to maintain your current results."
—Seth Whitted

During my second year of college, I had a neighbor who was into bodybuilding. He worked out every day and sometimes twice a day. He was educated on supplements and nutrition, and his upper body was super fit. His back, arms, and shoulders were cut up, and he managed to maintain a six pack. But one thing he hated was leg day. He despised leg day so much that he very rarely worked them out, and it showed. His body was disproportionate. This worked in his favor during the winter, but when it was time to pull the shorts out, we all knew he'd been skipping legs for months. I ran into him again during my senior year and was shocked to see he was skinny. He didn't look sick, but he definitely didn't have the same physical look he'd had a couple years prior. We chopped it up for a few minutes, and I asked him what happened. He said he fell off and didn't have much time to get to the gym like he used to.

I tell this story because I want you to realize that in all aspects of life, there is no such thing as maintaining progress, living on top, or remaining in your prime. In life, we're either progressing or we are slowly falling off. This is a brutal reality, but at the same time, it's liberating to know you can choose which direction you go in.

This reality also applies to mental health, emotional well-being, and personal battles. These areas of our lives are like muscles. We all have our own battles, but some are bigger than others. It doesn't really matter who has it worse or emotional health receives the focus, attention, and planning needed for progress. If your goal is to be physically fit, you must get in the gym and consistently work out, or your challenges will get the best of you.

In a 2016 article, licensed psychotherapist Sharon Martin suggests that people who focus more on their strengths are generally happier than people who don't.[2] Similarly, other psychologists state that it's important to put your energy into your strengths instead of your weaknesses to avoid stress and feel more satisfied in life.[3] I both agree

---

[2] Sharon Martin, "Using Your Strengths to Get Happier," PsychCentral, February 12, 2016, https://psychcentral.com/blog/imperfect/2016/02/using-your-strengths-to-get-happier.

[3] Michelle McQuaid, "Ten Reasons to Focus on Your Strengths," Psychology Today, November 11, 2014, https://

and disagree. I agree that we have to be careful about putting too much energy and focus on our weaknesses. For example, say a person is an impulsive spender and is always broke because of it. If they continue to talk about how they are not good with money, make jokes about having negative spending habits, or beat themselves up, they'll not only waste their time and energy, but their mindset can lead to them feeling depressed about the future of their finances. In my opinion, the only reason you should focus on your weaknesses is to create a solution for improvement. If your weakness is having a negative impact on your life, then it is important that you make a plan to improve in that area. Regardless, no one could ever convince me that completely ignoring your weaknesses is a good idea.

---

www.psychologytoday.com/us/blog/functioning-flourishing/201411/ten-reasons-focus-your-strengths.

There hasn't been much encouragement for black men in America to focus on our mental and emotional well-being. We've been taught to bury our pain, compartmentalize our struggles, and "be a man." But it doesn't just stop with men. Women have been told that they should get over the trauma they've gone through as well. No one actually teaches people how to assess what they're battling and improve those areas of their lives. Instead, we're taught to depend on medication to ease our hurt, which in my opinion is a ticking time bomb if you're not actively working on yourself in conjunction with the medication. Yes, therapy is available, but many people I know don't even consider it because of finances.

With this book, I hope to inspire you to create a playbook for the battles you're experiencing in your life, whether it's depression, abuse, anxiety, mental illness, or poor spending habits. Just know that you must take full ownership of your well-being because to give to others, you must first give to yourself.

You'll often hear top athletes talk about how they've improved their skills in the offseason, whether it's their strength, speed, or defense. The best of the best always have an improvement playbook. This is why your favorite player either gets better over time or slowly falls off. Your playbook should include a plan for expansion so you can add onto your strengths and control or remove your weaknesses. On my journey, I began having weekly business meetings with myself on either Saturday or Sunday to reflect on the previous week and measure my progress. During this meeting, I take the time to figure out where I fell short and what areas I need to improvement upon for the next week.

Here are a few steps you can take to develop a plan for yourself. First, in your notebook or digital journal, write down what areas of life you'd like to improve. This could be your impulsive decision-making, career, relationships, health, spirituality, mental well-being, or something else. Once you figure out your desired area of improvement, create two columns. On the right side, write out all the positives associated with this area of life. You could include your current strengths in this area, insights you've recently had, ways you've blessed others in this area, resources you've gathered, or the traits you possess that give you an advantage. Now, in the left column, write down all the negatives. This could include the habits that hinder your progress, the harmful actions you or others take, negative thoughts, or anything else that leads you toward the issues you don't want to deal with. Write as much as you can, and don't continue reading this book until you complete this exercise. Even if making this list takes you weeks, do what you've got to do.

Understand that finishing this list is not the end of the exercise. Not one human being is 100 percent aware of themselves. It might take you five years or longer to recognize most of your strengths and weaknesses, but if you ask a loved one, they may tell you something they've been trying to get through to you for years. It may hurt your feelings to realize something negative about yourself, but swallowing your pride and asking for help is a huge step in he right direction. Remember to surround yourself with loved ones who have your best interests at heart. Tell them hat you need their honest feedback in order to reach the goals you have for yourself. Give them time to share their thoughts and remind them that it is important that they are honest because if you don't know what to improve on, you an't be great. Some of you may have trust issues or a lackluster support system. In those cases, I would suggest seeking therapy or hiring a mentor who will be honest with you. If you still find yourself in a place without anyone to help you, then trust, isolation, and a negative perspective are probably some of your weaknesses. Go ahead and throw those on your list. If all else fails, praying can be a big help. The more I prayed for God to reveal my weaknesses, the quicker He showed them to me. Ask for your mental capacity to be expanded so you can see what you haven't been able to before. Ask for your eyes to be opened so you can serve Him better and achieve great things in life.

Once you have your list of strengths and weaknesses, put them in order of priority. Choose one strength and one area of improvement to work on at a time. It's important to narrow your focus as much as possible. Between your job, kids, school, business, and everything else life brings you, this process can become overwhelming. So, don't overdo it. Work with a sense of urgency and diligence, but don't overload yourself. Figure out a way to track your progress, whether it's data sheets, weekly or daily meetings, or an accountability partner. Please remember that this process is just like a muscle; don't think you can make small improvements then call it quits. This is something you'll need to work at for the rest of your life. It will take hard work, but over time, it will become second nature.

This process continues to change my life. You might be wondering how I developed this habit or how this turned into an important routine of mine. It all started back when I was in the fifth grade. My father was around, but he did not live with us, so I was raised by a single parent. Although my mother did an amazing job raising me, I missed out on the balance a two-parent home can provide.

Growing up in a home with only one parent has its pros and cons. I grew up close to my cousins; they were almost like brothers and sisters. But one of the cons was a lack of self-confidence. When I hung around my cousins, I always felt mentally and emotionally inferior, like their awareness and understanding of life was more advanced. The confidence they had when socializing was outstanding to me. I remember not being able to look people in the eyes for long periods of time. It's funny to think about now, but it was embarrassing at the time because I would beat myself up at night wondering why I felt anxious around other people. My cousins, on the other hand, carried themselves like adults. The way they were able to articulate their feelings, recall information under pressure, and listen attentively was mind-blowing to me.

My father lived two towns over and was very active in our lives. But not having a male figure in the house every day led to a lack of confidence for me. In my opinion, only a man can teach another man how to be confident as a man. I never knew whether my lack of confidence was because something was wrong with me, because I didn't have my father in the home, or because my cousins' strengths made me feel insecure and unable to change.

Another pro of my single-parent household was that it put a chip on my shoulder. I felt the need to prove myself, and that, mixed with my competitive spirit, turned my insecurities into a personal competition. I'm not sure if this was healthy or not, but it gave me a drive that was beyond human. I knew I had to figure out a way to keep up with everyone around me, then get ahead. This obsession used to keep me up at night. I remember hearing the quote "A woman can't raise no man," so I devised a plan. Please understand that I'm not trying to bash either of my parents. This was my younger self's way of taking full ownership of my future. I needed to make sure that I somehow figured things out.

Part of my plan was to pay close attention to every man I wanted to be like, whether it was my dad, my uncles, coaches, teachers, or local dope boys—basically anyone who drove a nice car or had jewelry. Yes, to a young man, toys equal success. My goal was to take the attributes I respected and implement them in my life. When I was faced with certain challenges, I would ask myself what they would do. The second part of my plan came about when I discovered the book of Proverbs. I consistently read scriptures, even if I couldn't understand them. I studied them day and night.

It wasn't until later in life that I realized I needed to consciously focus on my strengths as well. This was the beginning of me figuring out how to improve in the areas I fell short. This process helped me develop a strong sense of self-awareness and an awareness of my family as well. I started noticing both the positive and negative habits we had as a group. The positives are our loyalty to people, our giving spirit, our ability to listen and connect with people, and our faith. Some of the negative habits were like curses that caused cycles of poverty and health issues. I knew I had to make an impact.

This chapter is extremely important for your continuous growth. I charge you to become obsessed with improving yourself. Look back at the last ten to twenty years of your life and ask yourself how much you've grown personally. What negative habits have you overcome, and which ones are you still struggling to conquer? I believe there's a direct connection between self-improvement and an increase in opportunities. Look at it like this: the more you're capable of and the less you let things get in your way, the more you'll succeed at your goals.

"When life can trust you with ten, it'll throw you twenty." —Seth Whitted

7

OUTSMART YOUR ENVIRONMENT OR BECOME A PRODUCT OF IT

"The ones who think they are crazy enough to change the world are the ones who do."
—Steve Jobs

Josh Whisnant, a.k.a Whiz, is one of my best friends; I consider him a brother. He is the best example of this chapter's topic: outsmarting your environment. Whiz grew up in Pleasant View Projects (PV), one of five housing projects in the city we grew up in. Like most projects, it was filled with a lot of good-hearted people who were financially struggling. It's the type of struggle that teaches you how to survive with little to no resources, the type of survival that leads some down a path of crime. It's a place where many take pride in surviving their childhood, but few would actually want to stay and raise their children there.

Despite his environment not offering him much exposure to successful people who looked like him, Whiz always believed he would live a quality life. Even to this day, he'll remind you that he's putting in the work for his mother and sisters. You could be as pessimistic as you wanted, but you could never change his mind about how hard he was willing to work to make sure no family member of his went without. You're either inspired by his drive or you believe he is arrogant and you keep your distance. Whiz is a master at using the chip on his shoulder from his life experiences to fuel his drive, outwork anyone, and push himself no matter how hard things get. His drive for success has turned him into one of the best salesmen in America, and his current financial situation would seem unrealistic to a kid living in the same housing projects he came from. Sometimes I laugh when we're drinking together because he always brings up his blessings. But when I really think about it, he did something his environment didn't nurture him to do. He outsmarted it.

The way you view yourself and your capabilities to create a bright future plays a big role in where you'll end up. If you want to break a negative cycles and achieve success, you must first see yourself as a successful person in the present moment, no longer under the spell of the negative cycle your environment created.

POSITIVE MINDSET

Let's start by discussing how you can develop a better mindset. Before we begin, remember that this is not as easy as it sounds, especially when circumstances are stressful.

However, it's something you must go through to grow. The first step in cultivating a positive mindset is assessing your mindset to see if you currently view yourself and the world in a positive light. Second, you must figure out what made you think the way you do. And third, you must come up with a plan to develop or build upon your positive mindset.

I'm not even sure if Whiz realizes that he's always carried a positive view of himself. I'm sure his family had a lot to do with this. They are all positive people, and I was blessed to grow up around them. Whiz talked about what he was going to do so much that he unintentionally created affirmation statements or mantras. He did this naturally, way before today's influx of self-help gurus and law of attraction advocates. To him, a positive image of the future was crucial because he needed to be able to help his family.

According to The Psychology of Self-Affirmation (Steele, 1988) and studies conducted by Oxford University's

Social Cognitive and Affective Neuroscience journal, there is a connection between affirmations and our behaviors. How you view and speak about yourself in present and future tense plays a role in who you become. The way we view ourselves will determine whether or not we take an opportunity or turn it down. It is the difference between approaching that beautiful girl or convincing yourself that she's out of your league, the difference between taking back that abusive guy or telling yourself that you deserve a healthy, happy relationship.

"Whether you think you can or can't, you're right."
—Henry Ford

STEP 1: ASSESS YOUR MINDSET

Let's do step one together and evaluate how we see ourselves and the world around us. In addition to this exercise, I encourage you to go online and find tests that assess your underlying beliefs and general mindset. For right now, though, I challenge you to answer the following questions honestly and without judgment. For each question, give yourself one point for "never," two points for "sometimes/maybe," and three points for "always."

1. If a spouse, supervisor, or someone in a position of authority says, "We need to talk," do you get nervous and wonder what is wrong?
2. If the next step in your plans requires a solution that seems impossible to achieve, do you see that as a sign to move onto something else? (E.g. You want to buy a home, but the required down payment is an amount you've never had in your life.)
3. When you're reviewing a job listing, do the recommended qualifications keep you from filing

out the application because you believe they wouldn't want you?

4. Do you avoid flirting with extremely attractive people because you believe they are out of your league?
5. When people congratulate you or praise you for your hard work, do you deflect by giving the credit to others or saying it's no big deal?
6. Do you feel bad about succeeding at something because it may make others feel bad or insecure?
7. Do negative events ruin your entire day?
8. When someone does something that negatively affects you, do you spend a lot of time expressing your frustration and telling others how you were mistreated?
9. Do you believe it's inappropriate to find humor or enjoyment in the moment when something tragic

happens (e.g., death in the family, car accident)?

10. When negative things happen in your neighborhood (e.g., increase in housing prices or toxic tap water), do you believe a person or organization is purposely trying to sabotage the community?

Add up your points. These numbers can mean different things for different people, indicating anything from how you view life to how you approach new opportunities, self-care, or your environment. If your score is from ten to fifteen, you tend to have a positive perspective on life and are confident in yourself and your decisions. You most likely believe there's a logical reason behind everything and everyone's decisions. You tend to think more about solutions than problems, you can find enjoyment and humor in all situations, and you tend to lean toward a more positive self-image. You see the impossible as just another puzzle to figure out.

If you scored from sixteen to twenty-three, you're more of a balanced individual. You're likely a positive person most of the time, and you tend to put effort into remaining positive. Sometimes life events can get you down, but you are constantly working on yourself. Your mood can shift depending on the day and what's going on in your life. If your score is on the higher end of this range (twenty and up), you sometimes have moments that get the best of you, even though you know you should remain positive. You know your strengths and weaknesses, but you're hard on yourself more than you celebrate yourself.

If you scored between twenty-four and thirty, you tend to view life with a skeptical and critical eye. Others may often tell you to be more positive, but you believe you're just being realistic. You tend to find the negative in everything. It could be a beautiful sunny day, but to you, it's way too hot. Your job could give you a bonus check, but you'd be upset that the bonus put you in a higher tax bracket. You very rarely take risks because the potential negatives are a huge red flag to you.

If you're still uncertain about how you view yourself and the world, I challenge you to contact the support system you created back in chapter 2. Ask them if they see you as a positive or negative person. This step is extremely important. A lot of times people believe their worldview is correct when it's severely flawed. Take this seriously so you can uncover your true perspective.

STEP 2: WHAT SHAPED YOUR MINDSET?

Before we're able to have a positive mindset and view life as our playground, we must first understand how we developed the mindsets we carry today. I believe there are a number of factors that go into our personality and habits, including our genes and environment.

"Your environment is a perfect design to keep you exactly where you are."— Evan Carmichael

I love this quote by Evan Carmichael because it's the case for either a positive or negative mindset. According to Jacque Fresco, cofounder of The Venus Project, our environment shapes the way we think, act, feel, and take action. If you were a woman born in nineteenth-century China, you would likely act and think in a certain way than if you were born in the year 2000. Up until the 1950s, it was normal for Chinese women and girls to have their feet bound for aesthetic purposes. No matter how painful it was, people carried on with this tradition for more than a thousand years. Similarly, if you were born in a country where polygamy was normal, you likely wouldn't think twice about your father having multiple wives. In some families, it may also be normal for you to witness your father physically discipline your mother for what he perceived to be disrespect.

An example that hits home for me is the business of slavery in America. I use the word business because I want you to see it from that perspective for this example. In no way do I think slavery wasn't horrible. I just want you to look at it from a different perspective for a moment. In the seventeenth century, powerful individuals crafted a business model built on free labor that differed from those throughout history. In most countries, slavery consisted of one group of people conquering another and making them work against their will. It was typically driven by fear—whether fear of lost resources, poverty, or starvation—but fear was only a small portion of American slavery. These individuals knew that, eventually, everyone involved would view slavery as wrong, especially since America was deeply shaped by Christian moral truths. So to keep everyone's environment and mindset on one accord, they brainwashed enslaved people and both poor and rich whites. They convinced everyone, including black people themselves, that black people were born to be slaves, that, innately, they were less than human. This proved to be successful because otherwise good-hearted white people didn't attempt to end slavery; in their mind, it was justified. Enslaved people carried this mindset as well. Throughout our lives, we've learn about individuals, like Frederick Douglass, who thought differently, but he was a minority just like Whiz because Frederick knew how to read and was able to expand his mind. Only the wise and educated understood the evil strategy behind slavery. To everyone else, slavery was about racism.

It's tough to discuss the progression of the black community with both the conservative Republicans and liberal Democrats in America. Conservatives mostly believe that black people should simply take control of their lives and pull themselves up by their boot straps. Liberals look upon black folk with extreme pity, wanting to overhelp and make all the decisions for us. Both sides completely miss the real issue. It's not about money, a lack of help, laziness, or a lack of motivation. The issue is in the mindset, the way we view ourselves and the country and the way this country views us. In the black community, many of us still carry mindsets that are a symptom of the racism our family lines have endured, which perpetuates a cycle of terrible decision-making. This is why the "Just get over slavery" statement isn't profound because the mindsets we carry didn't stop at slavery. Black people were hosed down and lynched in the

’60s for wanting the right to vote. We’ve had to deal with the government flooding our communities with crack cocaine to fund an illegal war, the crime bill that followed that increased the prison population by 47 percent and removed an entire generation of parents from homes, welfare aid that unintentionally incentivized fathers to be absent from the home, unwarranted stop and frisks based on discriminatory practices, and so much more. I’m not sharing these facts for pity or to play the victim. I’m simply showing you why the average black person’s self-image isn’t so positive. You must truly understand how powerful mindset is to benefit from it, and most of our environments aren’t teaching us its power.

If you grew up around poverty and crime like my friends and I did, you likely didn’t realize how not normal our environment was. We grew up happy and loved, and we took pride in the city we came from. We had no clue we had deep-rooted mindsets and beliefs that could keep us in poverty and a life of crime. You often don't know you're in a negative cycle until someone exposes you to more and opens your eyes. According to the Office for National Statistics, more than half of adults who were abused as children experienced domestic abuse later in life.

In hindsight, it's easy to say that slavery was wrong and that black people should've rebelled or ran away. It's easy to say you wouldn't stay with an abusive partner, that you would be different if you grew up in poverty, that you wouldn't put up with domestic abuse. But when you're born into something, there's a big chance you will view those actions and habits as normal and go along with them.

Economic researchers conducted a study on adults who grew up in the 1980s. They found that only 50 percent of this group was earning more than their parents did at their age. The study also found that children who moved to a better environment improved their chances of reaching economic success. In fact, the earlier such a move took place, the greater the effect. So, you are more likely to become exactly what your environment represents. But there's also a small chance you could be among the minority, like Frederick Douglass and Whiz, and gain a different perspective that pushes you to change your circumstances.

I don't want to confuse anyone when I use the word environment. Sometimes this word makes us think of nature or the climate, but I'm talking about our personal environment, the day-to-day surroundings that influence us. This could include our family, neighborhood, work, education, favorite TV shows, social media platforms, and more. We have control over some of these things but not everything. I challenge you now to take a deep look at the environments that have nurtured you thus far. Pause your reading after this section and, in your notepad, assess how these environments have conditioned you and the people

\around you for good or bad. Write down the negatives and positives of your environment. Then, ask people who have experienced a similar environment for their perspective. Especially talk to the people who have excelled at a high level, like Whiz.

Once you've figured out how your environment has or still cultivates your habits, mindsets, and life perspectives, it's time to actually change these perceptions and mindsets.

STEP 3: DEVELOP A POSITIVE MINDSET AND SELF-IMAGE

The first step is to understand that this is not a one-time fix. Changing your mindset is an ongoing process. I'm not saying it's going to be easy, but it's a must. You are about to transform an entire life's worth of ways that you unknowingly or knowingly have. Matthew 9:17 says, "And no man put new wine into old bottles; else the new wine will burst the bottles, and be spilled, and the bottles shall perish. But new wine must be put into new bottles; and both are preserved."

Your attitude and mindset are easily measured when you start paying close attention to these four areas in your life: your thoughts, emotions, the words you speak, and the actions you take.

PROGRAMMING YOUR THOUGHTS Programming yourself to have positive thoughts is difficult and requires consistency. One of the most important things I do to program my thoughts is start my day learning useful information, whether it's in the form of a book, podcast, Facebook video, or music. Imagine what it would be like to wake up and have every person you looked up to follow you throughout your day. Imagine the conversations you'd have, the mental space they'd put you in, how much information they'd drop on you, and what you'd do with your day because of it. You would be a machine that was driven to make anything happen. Well, you can achieve that level of determination by simply typing their names into YouTube and listening to one of their interviews while you get ready for the day. Sometimes I read through my daily goals in the morning to remind myself of what needs to be done. This also puts me in a mental space to be productive and think about positive things. Above all else, find a way to start your morning on the right foot.

The hardest part of changing your mindset is dealing with those other friends friends that want to hang out in the morning, the friends that tell you you ain't shit or the ones who tell you to check social media. These are most often the people who remind you that focusing on your goals is too hard or tiring. They'll want to start debates with people who aren't in the room about subjects that aren't relevant. I may be alone in this, but my thoughts have always run wild. I had to learn to not entertain distracting or irrelevant thoughts. I literally have to fight the urge to argue with myself. I kid you not, I sometimes have full-blown, twenty-minute arguments with someone who isn't eve in the room. So I began either finishing my thoughts on paper or cutting it off and looking at my list again to refocus myself. Medication is not an option for me. I want to work on my mind like it's a muscle, so I've downloaded focus-based, memory, and brain-building games, like chess. I used to do these early in the morning to remind myself of how focused I needed my mind to be during the day. It wasn't easy to rearrange my thoughts, but it was necessary.

If positive thinking is one of your goals, make a decision to do something every day that will help keep you positive. Don't make it too overwhelming. It could be reading an informative book for five minutes, journaling, praying, or meditating—whatever works best for you. For me, what worked best was putting on headphones and pressing play on one of the many audiobooks I'm listening to. Reminding myself of my weekly goals also works to focus my mind.

CHANGE HOW YOU FEEL

Now, let's discuss your feelings. This could possibly be the most difficult thing to change because it's tough to step outside of yourself and what you're feeling. To reach your goals in any aspect of life, you must control how you react to and feel about things. I truly enjoy being present through any circumstance, and I do mean any circumstance.

Before my mother passed in 2019, we were extremely close. She was a beautiful, selfless, inspiring master of survival who continues to motivate me, even in death. Right before she passed, the doctor called down to the hospital's visitor room where my sister Tonette and I were sleeping. He said he didn't believe my mother would make it through the night and that it was time to say goodbye. We immediately called Aunt Pess (my mom's sister), Unc Mob (her brother), and my brother Ascheley to let them know what the doctor had to say. They all rode up to the hospital, hoping to get there before she passed away. My sister and I sat in the room with her and prayed for God to heal my mother in the way we know only He can. About forty minutes later, everyone arrived. We prayed, held her hand, kissed her warm forehead, and took in her scent. My sister asked me to read a specific scripture, and as soon as I finished, my mom's heart rate began to drop. The doctors asked us to step out while they tried to revive her. After a few minutes, they brought us back in to say our goodbyes. Her battle with cancer started roughly four weeks prior, when she went to the hospital with some pain. I remember her saying she was going to beat it and that she was going to fight. That's all I could think about as I stood there kissing her warm forehead. I looked at my aunt, sister, and brother and said, "Man, I'm so proud of her. She banged until the end." I started laughing out of amazement.

An unexplainable amount of peace came over me, and I was able to step outside of myself. I recognized that I, and everyone else, was hurting, but I was at peace. I remembered how my grandmother's death tore a hole in my mother's heart and how it took her years to recover. She was irritable, isolated herself from the family, and experienced depression. She even made us cancel the birthday party we were trying to throw her. I knew I didn't want that for us, and I knew she wouldn't want that either, so I decided to speak with everyone before we left the hospital so we could find a way to grieve in a healthy way. A few minutes after my mother died, I was online researching grief and PTSD. What

I learned in a few minutes was that there is no perfect way to grieve, but if you don't grieve in a healthy way, you can create a storm that's hard to come back from.

Before leaving the hospital, I said to everyone, "There is no right way to grieve, but there sure is a wrong way. All of our lives, people have told us to be strong and not cry. I remember how much Grandma's death affected Mom, and I know she wouldn't want that for us. So, fuck being strong. When you feel like crying, embrace it to the fullest. Don't avoid the pictures and videos. Go to those familiar places. Let's dive head first into this. Letting it all out is the real strength."

I challenged my brother and sister to write about how they were feeling every day. I would drive to my mom's job and visit her house. I would put myself in every situation to feel the burn of the loss. I didn't want to bury or compartmentalize anything. And it worked. We were at so much peace that when the funeral came, my siblings and I all participated. My brother spoke, I sang a song, and my sister preached a sermon. Yes, it was the hardest performance I've ever done, but looking back, it was unbelievable how we were able to maneuver the way we did days after our mother had died.

I was able to celebrate her life, find humor in the moment, and enjoy people's company during the week of her funeral and after. That was all a result of years of working with God to cultivate mindfulness. He showed me the path, and I practiced every day. People at my job can't understand how I'm able to point out the positives or find humor in stressful moments, but this is a skill that comedians have developed throughout their careers. Developing this skill set gives you a superpower that not many people have. While everyone else is emotional, panicking, or stressed out, you can be at peace and see the opportunities, solutions, and other useful perspectives. So, I challenge you to find the positives in every situation, no matter how small they may be, and create a different perspective

How you feel on a daily basis is important as well. I believe one of the many gifts that God has given us is the power of faith. I'm not talking about faith in the way traditional religions teach you. I'm talking about the faith Jesus and every other great person who has walked this earth has embodied. The way we feel is a key ingredient in this process. You have to think, speak, and feel the things you want.

"Then he touched their eyes, saying 'According to your faith, let it be to you.'" (Matthew 9:29, NKJV)

"Then Jesus said to the centurion, 'Go your way; and as you have believed, so let it be done for you.' And his servant was healed that same hour." (Matthew 8:13, NKJV)

What a lot of teachers of the Word do not speak about is how Jesus had to get people to "think, act, and feel" as if they were already healed and fully accept said healing for it to work. This is what happened when the woman who had blood issues for twelve years touched the hem of his garment and said within herself that she may be made whole. Jesus turned to her and said, "Your faith has made you whole." He pointed out that her faith was so strong, she was able to heal herself.

It's pointless to say "I am healed" when, deep in your gut, you don't really feel like you're going to be healed. It's like saying "My business will be funded," but then you don't move forward with any plans. We have to focus on what it'll feel like to obtain the things we want and pray for. Any distractions will wipe out that faith Jesus was trying to teach us. Don't believe me? Look what happened when he was in his hometown. Really put yourself in the people of Nazareth's shoes. When Jesus traveled to faraway places, the people who didn't know him personally were curious and eager to be healed. But in his hometown, they knew him as Little Joseph, the carpenter, the child of the crazy Mary chick who convinced Joseph that she didn't cheat and the baby was God's. I honestly feel bad that they had to grow up with him because they knew him before the transformation. They knew the good, the bad, and the ugly about him. To the people of Nazareth, Jesus was a normal person just like them.

He went away from there and came to his hometown, and his disciples followed him. And on the Sabbath, he began to teach in the synagogue, and many who heard him were astonished, saying, "Where did this man get these things? What is the wisdom given to him? How are such mighty works done by his hands? Is not this the carpenter, the son of

Mary and brother of James and Joseph and Judas and Simon? And are not his sisters here with us?" And they took offense at him. And Jesus said to them, "A prophet is not without honor, except in his hometown and among his relatives and in his own household." And he could do no mighty work there, except that he laid his hands on a few sick people and healed them. And he marveled because of their unbelief. (Mark 6:1–6, ESV)

Let's not overlook the part that says, "and He could do no mighty work there." The people of Nazareth were so consumed with their ideas of him and the fact that they knew him and his family that they couldn't hear his messages. Imagine your childhood best friend one day tells you they're the son of God. You're going to laugh or think they have a mental disability. Their thoughts, feelings, words and actions were consumed so much that they couldn't receive any messages. And verse 5 says ' and he could do no mighty work there'. Really think about that. We were always taught that Jesus was different from us, even though he said we would do greater things. His sacrifice was bigger than him dying on the cross. The other part to the sacrifice was that he was also in flesh form, and flesh comes with its demons. Jesus became perfect because he was able to master himself and use the Kingdom of God within him to do many wonderful things. Because of the way we are taught today, we often miss the message that our power is held in how we think, feel, speak, and act.

There's a deeper level to how we feel. Deep within you, on a subconscious level, there are feelings you may or may not be aware of. Your subconscious beliefs are the ones that held deep down that have been shaped by your religion, culture, and family. The average person feels some level of guilt or shame about something, which can lead to stress, anxiety, and depression, and Christianity has a way of perpetuating this for a lot of people. For some reason, we were taught that success, money, and earthly happiness was somehow wrong, and that struggling was virtuous, God-like, and a symbol of strength. So most of my life, I felt guilty about wanting money and experiencing good things. Looking back now, this was how most people I knew felt. I would literally hide the good things that happened to me out of guilt and shame, knowing there were others in the world who were going through hard times. In a weird way, I actually felt better when bad things happened because then no one could get offended.

Putting religious teachings aside, people sometimes feel like they don't deserve happiness or success because of their past wrongdoings. In chapter 5, we discussed consequence, but to be clear, accepting your consequences and feeling like you don't deserve good things are two different things. Accepting your consequences helps you move forward and learn from your mistakes, and a big part of moving forward involves forgiving yourself and vowing to never make those mistakes again.

Jen Oliver, the CEO of FitMama, stated that most women feel guilt and shame right after having a baby because, at that moment, all they can think about is getting back in shape the way society tells them to. She says it's hard for women to be in the moment with their child because of the shame of how their body looks. Psychologists have also pointed to guilt as a reason why it's so hard for women to lose weight after pregnancy. After my wife had baby Story, she worked hard for months to get back in shape. She watched a TikTok that told her to be OK with her changing body and feel her beauty regardless. Once she removed those feelings of shame and guilt from her daily life, her body weight started dropping naturally.

You must change your deep beliefs if you want to succeed at anything. You have to turn your feelings of guilt into a sense of entitlement. You need to truly feel like you deserve success, happiness, and prosperity. Forgive yourself for the wrong you've done because holding onto that guilt and shame will only rob you from living in the moment. I'm not saying you shouldn't be critical of your decisions and lifestyle. I'm stating that you deserve to be happy, prosperous, and proud of who you are while continuing to work toward becoming a better version of yourself. This part is crucial because if you don't feel worthy of happiness, then you will not achieve it. You must fully enjoy the journey of your life. So, be fulfilled right now. Don't react shamefully when someone compliments you. Don't call yourself ugly when someone says you're beautiful. Don't downplay your skills because you feel shy. Stop it! The answer is to fully love yourself now and love the journey of improving too.

So, I challenge you to become aware of how you feel in every area of your life, whether it's health, wealth, or family. The way you feel about yourself writes your future, so no matter what the circumstances are, you need to do what makes you happy.

Take a moment here to ask yourself if you deserve the things you want to accomplish. Pay attention to the deep-rooted feelings that come up and explore them. Ask yourself why you feel the way you do. For example, when I talk about Whitted Media being a billion-dollar company, I say, "I can do it," but deep down, there's doubt. When I explore that doubt, I realize that it's due to my past mistakes with leadership, money management, and a lack of execution. In that moment, my subconscious mind is completely ignoring all my successes and is choosing to hold onto the shame I felt after I fell short. Write a list of why you deserve to accomplish your goals and what you plan to do to not make the mistakes of your past again. Anytime you feel unworthy, re-read this list and explore your deep rooted feelings. Again, write down why you deserve success and what you plan to do to protect yourself against feeling that guilt and shame.

If you want happiness, you must listen to, read, and watch things that make you happy. If you want to be healthy, you must imagine what that would feel like. Once you grasp these feelings, meditate on them until you accept that they are your reality. Yes, I'm asking you to be slightly delusional! If you're homeless sleeping under a bridge, I'm telling you to feel abundance, think abundance, and take action that feels abundant. When I was at my worst, I took time out of the day to imagine myself in a better position. Even now, when I am happier and feeling more fulfilled, I meditate daily on my goals, including one day running Whitted Media full-time. During this meditation, I pray and tell myself that i will quit my Job by March of 2022. I've only got 9 months until that point. I make myself feel what it will be like, and I attempt to stay in that feeling for as long as possible. So if you're reading this book after March 2022, message me to see if I'm running the company full time.

The hardest part of this process is becoming aware of how you're feeling and changing these emotions. This is where journaling comes in. Write out how you feel during a moment of discomfort and why, then ask yourself how you want to feel instead. From there, develop a process that will help you change your feelings. For some, that'll involve music, reading, talking to a funny or inspiring friend, or painting. Ask God to show you a process that will help you let go of the wrong feelings and welcome in the right ones. Expressing how you feel isn't a problem, but allowing those negative feelings to consume you is, so address them then transform them into something productive.

Have you ever seen someone walk in the room and you instantly knew they were powerful? People will treat them well, give them information, or try to impress them. I guarantee, in that moment, they felt powerful too. The way someone feels and acts will determine how others view and treat them. So, feel entitled to the things you want, carry that with you everywhere you go, and you'll start to notice the right people and circumstances surrounding you. You'll feel confident enough to talk to the bank about that business idea, and you'll feel more secure in your decisions.

CHANGE YOUR ENVIRONMENT

One of the biggest challenges when it comes to changing our thoughts, perspectives, actions, and feelings is our environment. It's extremely important that you change your environment to one that is in alignment with what you want out of life. This was tough for me, so I'm going to break down my environment into categories to show how each aspect affected me and how I changed my circumstances.

CAREER

I wanted to become a successful entrepreneur and artist, but my environment only knew poverty. There wasn't anyone around I could look up to. The majority of us came from hardworking families who lived paycheck to paycheck. The people who were successful were always busy, so we never saw them. The only people we saw on a daily basis who appeared to be successful were drug dealers and some sports coaches. My mother, who I love dearly, had little to no knowledge on financial literacy and had terrible money management skills, but she was a master of survival.

So as a result, my finances were up and down until my thirties. My career consisted of selling drugs, working dead-end jobs, and chasing a dream with no real plan.

Although I conquered some goals and made some great memories, I ultimately failed in this department.

HEALTH

I can't speak for all black folks in America, but the culture of my environment involved indulging in high-sodium, greasy food that was terrible for our health and neglecting to exercise, believing instead that all of our health and weight issues are passed down in the family. Growing up, I only saw the men in my family and sports coaches working out, and they were generally the only ones who encouraged us kids to do the same. Because of this food culture and mindset toward exercise, my family experienced fourteen deaths between 1997 to 2007. Most of them were due to heart issues and overall bad health.

So, for a good portion of my life, I ate for taste and worked out to remain in shape. The amount of deaths in our family led the younger generations to figure out what changes we needed to make to live healthier lives. When Google and YouTube came out, we started looking into healthier eating and lifestyle choices and inspired the rest of our family. But this was still met with resistance from the rest of the community. They say we eat like white people. Yes, healthy eating in the black community is looked at as "eating like white people" and selling out.

FAMILY AND RELATIONSHIPS

I grew up around inspiring people who loved each other and were extremely loyal. My family members who were married showed us what a healthy marriage looked like, but there were also those who created broken homes by having children out of wedlock or cheating on their spouse. My father, who I love dearly, had children with two different women back to back. My sister was born in January of 1986, my stepbrother was born in February of 1987, and I was born in March of 1987. Most of the men in my community only talked about sleeping with women and who looked good or not.

Overall, I feel like I was blessed to grow up in the tight-knit family I was raised in, especially because they always pushed us to become better than they were. Family is everything to me. I consider my closest friends as family too. I'm extremely loyal, and I care about everyone in my life.

In my younger years, I was mainly focused on having sex with women. I built connections with them so I could get all the benefits of a relationship without actually committing to one. I only had one serious relationship before I met my wife. I followed what I thought was an honor code. I would only get in a relationship if I didn't plan on messing around with other chicks, which is why I was single the majority of the time. But there was no honor in sleeping around because I was wasting everyone's time. When I settled down, I had no idea how to be a good partner, let alone a husband. It's all been a learning process, and I'm aware that I have a lot more learning to do.

SPIRITUAL

I grew up in a spiritual, churchgoing family. We came together to pray anytime someone was in need or was dealing with an issue. I was taught to consult God for everything. As a result, I have a tight relationship with the Creator. I'm not much of a churchgoer at the moment, but I continuously study the principles of God and His Son and apply them to my life.

As a poor kid living in a rough environment, I was determined to overcome my circumstances and figure out a way to change everything. Naturally, I've always been an observer and a listener, but this is hard to do when you don't have access to people who can take you where you want to o. But everything changed in January 2006. In the computer lab at my college, my homie Mar showed me a video on YouTube called "Joey Jihad Knockout." It was a ideo of a guy from Philly who was rapping one moment, hen got knocked out and robbed the next. I remember laughing as he told me we could look up anything on the website. To test his theory, I said, "Look up lion videos." He laughed, put it in the search bar, and an entire page of lion videos came up. A light bulb went off in my head.

I realized at that moment that I could look up any question I'd ever had; information was literally at my fingertips. I felt like I could do anything with enough research. If I needed to perform heart surgery, I could look up videos and instruction manuals and get you that new heart. It might skip a few beats every now and then, but I'll get it in!

So, how did this discovery help me change my environment? Whatever influence I couldn't find in my neighborhood, I found it online. For example, when I was making music, I knew I needed to understand the business side of it more and surround myself with others who had experience. I couldn't find those kinds of people in my immediate environment, so I went online and watched interviews, behind-the-scenes footage, and documentaries and read books written by industry folks. I would surround myself with people, like Jay-Z, Kanye, LA Reid, and Dame Dash. By doing this, I felt like I was always receiving advice. Jay would remind me to focus on sales, Kanye would encourage me to be different, and Dame would berate me for wasting time and push me to be more productive.

I realized I could change my environment without physically affecting it. It takes a little imagination, study, and discipline to consume the right content and take what you need from it. The hard part is recognizing what environment you really need. When I first started, I consumed any and everything. All this did was turn me into a conspiracy theorist. I'm not saying there isn't any truth to any conspiracies because I can see past all the BS we're taught, but I realized that wasn't my route. So, first, you have to know where you're headed and recognize what information serves you, and then you need to figure out what environment you need to surround yourself with. I wasted a lot of time consuming unnecessary content. You don't have to do that. Be specific. If you want to develop your financial literacy skills, then look up information about investing and saving and listen to the stories of people who have come from similar circumstances. If you want to break the cycle of abusive relationships, then read up on healthy relationships, follow the stories of people who are in them, and listen to TED Talks by therapists who work with clients on this every day.

Another way to change your environment is by meeting new people. It's easy to build relationships with people who think and act just like you, but it's difficult to build relationships with people who are different from you. It's hard to connect with someone if you have nothing in common with them. Imagine working a dead-end serving job at Applebee's, but you want to build a relationship with the CEO. You'll most likely have nothing in common with them, and you'll probably look at life differently. The conversation would most likely end in awkward silence. I'll tell you from personal experience how I build relationships with people who have the knowledge to change my life.

One of the ways I've built relationships with people is by adding value to their life and situation. When I meet someone, I ask as many questions as I can. I'm genuinely interested in people, and the more I hear about them and what they do, the more I think about how I can provide value to them. I don't go into any situation thinking about what I can take or get in return. I simply just add value. That could be information, a lead, a connection to another colleague, or a critique that could change their lives. This dynamic builds a natural relationship over time. Every now and then, I may have a question or need some advice, and this person could point me in the right direction or introduce me to someone who can help. So, build up a reputation of adding value to others and doing things with the right intentions and you'll build a network that is priceless. My boy Wells is great at this. When I first got to know him, his character stood out to me. As the years went on, he always reached out with information or a connection. I can count on one hand the amount of times he's asked me for anything, but I can't count how many connections, resources, and pieces of advice he's given me. I can only imagine what his network is like these days.

Another way you can connect with people is to be a coachable student. Most successful people love to share knowledge and information, and they hate keeping it all to themselves. The problem is they don't want to speak if their words aren't going to be valued. Imagine spending an hour giving someone advice only for them to do the opposite of what you told them. That's a slap in the face because you could've used that hour to do something else. Also when you get around smarter and successful people, SHUT UP! Most people think they have to impress successful people with big words or fascinating stories, but when it's time to learn, you have to shut up and listen because you'll most likely only have a limited amount of time with them. Let that person give you all the gems they have to offer. Don't try to prove your worth with fancy words; prove yourself by taking their advice and succeeding with it. If you show them you can apply the information they give, they will pour more into you. There is nothing more gratifying than being able to help someone level up.

So, when you find a potential mentor, let them know that you want to learn and you will not waste their time. You may need to pay them and book a consultation the first few times to get their attention, but if they know you're willing to put money behind yourself, they may take you seriously and give you the gems you need at no cost.

One of the first times I did this was with Nate Giles. I saw he was working with Roc Nation and had a sit-down with Gary Vee, so I had to see what this dude was doing and how I could replicate it for myself. Giles and I are the same age, and we come from rival towns. Most people would let that kind of thing get in the way, but I was not about to let pride get in the way of my progress. I reached out to him and told him I was willing to pay for a consultation. He told me I didn't need to pay him and that he would be in town soon so we could chop it up.

When we met, he said, "I'm not gonna lie, you got everything it takes, from talent to story, but I can tell you just make music to be the best and that's it." It messed me up because I wanted to say, "Of course, why not?" but I know that when someone is further along than you, you need to listen. So I replied, "What do you mean?" He told me that talent is important, but that my goals and intentions are even more important. "I can tell you make great music, then you just promote and promote and make good music again," he said.

I was still shocked because I couldn't see anything beyond that. I always thought having talent and outworking everyone was the key to success, but I was wrong. I replied, "What would you do if you were in my shoes?"

"I would set goals outside of just views and releases,"

he said. "Let me just give you an example. Did you see the interview I did with Gary Vee? Well, that was a goal I set. Everything I did was with the intention of reaching that goal. I followed Gary on everything and turned on notifications so when he tweeted, I would see it first. I waited months for an opportunity. Then one day, Gary posted his new shoes. I quickly tweeted back telling him I would buy fifteen pairs of shoes for fifteen minutes of his time. He tweeted back saying he'll give me five minutes for fifteen pairs of shoes, and I agreed. He tagged his assistant and told him to set up an appointment when I showed the receipt. Long story short, I set a goal and reached it. You need to start doing that with music. Set goals for the big articles, shows, and features you want. When you show fans the things you're doing, they'll become excited and support you more. So many people have been messaging me since I posted that pic with Gary Vee. I also learned a lot from him.

So, set big goals and do everything you can to reach them."

With that one conversation, Giles not only changed how I'd approach things moving forward, but he opened a can of worms regarding my upbringing and mentality. At that moment, I realized I was raised to be a master of defense, but I wasn't taught how to play good offense. But the conversation wouldn't have happened at all if I wasn't coachable and willing to invest in his time, if I was too prideful because he was the same age as me or from a rival town.

So, I challenge you to become aware of your environment. Make sure you develop a personal environment that helps you reach your goals. I encourage you to become aware of your mindset, the thoughts you have, the words you speak, the feelings you express, and the way you view yourself and your actions. Take all of these things into account and determine what you're going to put your faith into. This is what Jesus was trying to teach us. He told us we would do greater things than him. Once we can direct all of these faith tools toward our purpose and goals, we can achieve anything. Don't become distracted like the people of Nazareth.

Now, take a minute to pause here and ask yourself what you want to accomplish. Research the people who have achieved these goals and either make a goal to have a conversation with them or read their books and watch their interviews. The goal isn't to be just like them; the goal is to see what habits helped them achieve their goals, then figure out how you can apply these things to your life. Surround yourself with these people, and you'll start to notice positive changes.

8
MASTER OF DEFENSE BUT NO OFFENSE

"Defense is important, but without offense, you can burn yourself out. Without offensive strategies and plays, you can never get ahead."
—Seth Whitted

February in Pennsylvania is cold. So cold that I often wonder why we torture ourselves by living here. The February cold is even worse if the gas in your house goes out because no gas means no heat. Growing up, there were a number of times the utilities went out in the house because of unpaid bills. As a single parent, sometimes things get tight or one bill has to be sacrificed for something else. Maybe there's an event or a sport at school that my mom didn't want us to miss out on. My father was still in the picture when it came to finances, but my mother was a prideful woman at times.

Looking back, I don't remember being sad during these moments. It was actually the opposite. We were always ready to kick things into survival mode at any point. We were locked and loaded for hard times. My mother made sure to arm us for trials and tribulations. She would regularly call meetings in her bedroom and break things down to us, from what the problem was to how we were going to handle it.

"The heat is going to go out, so this is what we're going to do to handle this situation and survive," my mother would say as we gathered around her bed.

As a child, I remember saying to myself, "This ain't shit. Let's go. We got this. You got your warm clothes for sleeping."

We'd have a big pot of spaghetti ready to go into the microwave, cereal, and sandwich fixings. I respect my mother for never letting the hard times break us, and I take pride in my ability to weather any storm without letting it negatively affect me or spill over into another area of life. Even when there was a death or illness in the family, we were able to lock in and rise to the occasion. We would use the pain from that hard time as our driving force to outperform others. Even to this day, I can still lock into this mode and outwork anyone, even my past self. My friend Tyjack calls it "that dog."

I have my mother to thank for that dog. That was our defense, and we were great at playing it. I respect you, Mom, and I thank you for teaching us defense. I vow to take it to the next level. From the outside looking in, most people would think my mother mismanaged her funds or had a lack of discipline. But when you're a single parent raising children in a high-crime environment, when addiction runs in the family, and when your neighborhood threatens to take your children under, you don't have time to think about anything except surviving those conditions. That's why I am determined to expand on my mother's teachings and make her proud. One of the ways I took her guidance to the next level was by realizing my family only played defense, which led to us hoping to win but eventually losing. When we had an easier time, like during tax season when bills were paid and there was a little financial cushion, we would go shopping, relax, or do anything to enjoy the moment and take a load off because we'd just dealt with multiple hard times back to back, which is extremely exhausting.

One day I was doing some research on how to market a music project, and in the video the person said the difference between rich people and poor people is that rich people make things happen and poor people let life happen to them. This sounds so basic, but it made me realize that, yes, we were masters of defense, but when it was time to play

offense, we didn't have any plays. There was no vision to get ahead and actually win. I think a lot of people, especially those of us who come from a poor culture, play defense and never play offense. I believe people don't make offensive plays because they either misuse moments of comfort, attempt to hold on to the money they have, have a negative perspective of financial success, or they're trying to be perfect.

Just to be clear here are some examples of offense and defense. Defense is when a problem happens you work to get yourself out of that situation. This could be your car breaking down, health issues, bills getting backed up, issues in your home that require you to come up with a large sum of money and any other situation that forces you to come up with a plan to get yourself out of the current circumstance.

Playing offense is implementing a strategy to get ahead in a specific area in your life. Offensive strategy is something that people from all walks of life can partake in.

This could be furthering your education in your area of expertise in order to grow your business. Starting business account and forcing yourself to add $100 a month so that when a future investment opportunity presents itself, you will have the funds to invest. Researching health and fitness, putting a exercise and diet plan together for yourself in order to get in shape and prevent health issues is also playing offense. Artist and entreprenuers will set goals for expanding the customer base by hiring a mentor or reading a book to expand their knowledge and expertise. Any act of putting a detailed plan together with the intentions of progressing in any area of your life is considered offense. Playing offense looks different for everyone. A poor persons offense will most likely be a plan focused on reaching financial freedom. A rich person offense might involve putting a plan together to expand the business.

MISUSING MOMENTS OF COMFORT

After going through a rough patch, it's normal for parents to want their children to feel like kids and have a moment of enjoyment. So when they get a little money, they often plan a trip or outing or buy them some new clothes. This isn't just limited to parents and kids, though. Let's say you just got out of a bad relationship and you want to understand why things didn't go well and how you can improve and find a better partner next time. There's so much research, self-evaluating, and improvement that needs done, but comfort says you should relax and do nothing. A few weeks go by and you find someone new without doing any work on yourself. Eventually that relationship goes bad too, and you're back in the same position thinking that love isn't for you or that there are no good partners around.

The problem with comfort is that the world will

continue to move forward, even if you're not. Don't get me wrong; taking some time to relax after going through hard times, like death, abuse, or financial hardship, is needed. So take some time for yourself, but in order to grow, there needs to be some focus on improvement. Opportunities don't care about what you just went through nor will they wait on you. So you can kick your feet up or you can get to work.

We know our bodies need to rest, which means that roughly eight hours of our day are already accounted for. What you do with the sixteen hours you have left determines whether you are progressing or slowly falling off. Imagine going to the gym and eating healthy every day for three years and getting amazing results. What do you think would happen if you stopped going to the gym? Would your muscles stay the same, or would you lose all your progress?

Remember, comfort is the killer of advancement. I'm not telling you not to rest, but you should find brief moments of comfort, set goals, and not let the desire to be comfortable stop you from reaching them.

ATTEMPTING TO HOLD ONTO THE MONEY YOU HAVE

Making plays can cost money, time, or both. And because people are often afraid their money will run out, they try to hold onto it for as long as possible. In the past, I used to hold onto money with the intentions of saving or growing it, but in life, there is always a need for money, and that need usually comes in the form of an emergency. I'm not trying to be pessimistic; I just understand that there's always an emergency that is ready to wipe out all the money you're trying to hold on to. If it's not your emergency, then it'll be a loved one who is in a jam.

Making plays enables you to put that money and time somewhere safe to either avoid emergencies altogether or take care of them quickly. For example, my boy Felo got locked up and needed to sell his Cadillac to pay his lawyer. Another friend was selling a two-door truck for $800. The car wasn't running and needed some work, and since my cousin Mob and I had been buying and selling cars for a while, we decided to partner. Felo only asked for $1,200 and said he would accept four payments. I was in a jam at the moment, but I went for it. Mob grabbed the bumper and painted it, and the mechanic we took it to didn't charge us much to get it running. It was also tax season, and the Cadillac had twenty-inch rims and a TV monitor in it. Kelley Blue Book estimated it was worth between $4,000 and $7,000, so we posted it on Craigslist and someone purchased it for $4,500. At the same time, someone else on the site was selling a truck for the same price, so I made an agreement similar to theirs. That truck didn't need any work, and the Blue Book estimate was the same. I sold that car during tax season as well.

On the surface, these sound like easy decisions, but they weren't. My personal vehicle wasn't inspected and was overheating due to a bad gasket, I needed that initial $300 for the Cadillac, and I had no clue what was wrong with it. So, I made those deals with little to no money, and I sold both during tax season when my own car was damn near broken down. After splitting profits with Mob, I had about $6,000 to work with. My personal vehicle completely broke down after that, but I had already used some of the money as a down payment for a new car. Imagine if I had tried to hold onto that little $300 I had in the beginning.

So, I encourage you to consider the long-term benefits of investing. The more research you do and the more you understand, the more peace you'll have. I don't recommend spending your money blindly or emotionally, but I do encourage you to fight against the fear of failure.

NEGATIVE PERSPECTIVE TOWARD IDEAS

There are many people who have been through so much negativity in their lives that they can't even believe something good will come from their hands. These people wait for their boss or someone else to either bless them or provide a plan that feels safe and comfortable.

In chapter 7, we talked about how damaging these feelings of unworthiness can be. This is often a tough mindset for people to change because the way they view the world and themselves is law in their mind, and until they can become aware of the connection between their beliefs and their decisions, they will continue to unknowingly perpetuate the same cycles over and over. Don't wait on someone else to tell you that you deserve success. Even if you don't believe it right now, act as if you do, and soon enough, you will.

THE PERFECTIONIST

In my opinion, the majority of smart or talented people have a habit of perfectionism. To them, it's never the right time to do something because things aren't lined up absolutely perfectly. My boy Seth Job is one of the smartest people I know, but he knows too much to believe in anything. If you bring a great idea up to him, he will provide a legitimate reason for why it won't work. He'll either say there are other options out there or there's a missing piece of the puzzle. I enjoy bringing ideas to him because I know he'll find the holes in them. To me, the hole symbolizes what I can work on, but for Job, the hole symbolizes why the plan will not work. I'm a delusional, optimistic dreamer, and I'm OK with it. I'm willing to do as much research as I can up front and figure the rest out little by little as I continue on the journey. This is why the dumbest and least talented people will sometimes succeed. They weren't smart enough to realize that it wouldn't work, so they went for it anyway.

Imagine only playing defense in a game of basketball. The other team shoots, you get the rebound, run to the other end of the court,pass the ball around and take a shot before l the shot clock runs out. Growing up, we often decided to take a break because playing defense is extremely hard work.

A lot of us who come from a poor environment have a misconception that struggle is something that only happens to poor people. Many people believe that rich folks have all the right resources or wealthy parents, and they don't have to put in effort for anything. This is not always true. Everything you do comes with struggle, whether it's starting a business, clocking in at your nine-to-five, or going to school. Making offensive struggle a normal occurrence is the key to a better life.

So, to take my defensive teachings to the next level, I

started reminding myself what my long-term goals were, and I began making offensive plays every single day no matter what. Once I started doing that, growth felt inevitable. And guess what? I still have to play defense every now and then, but the difference now is that defense doesn't feel so rough. Mom, I hope you're proud of me for breaking the cycle and sticking to my vow.

Just a few months ago, my wife's car broke down, my truck's engine light was on, my spending account was at zero, bills were due, and a pipe had burst in my bathroom, flooding the entire first floor and basement, including my podcast equipment. On top of all that, COVID made it hard to expand my media business the way I had planned. Can you picture what I'm saying? My home flooded, all of the video and audio equipment I invested in was damaged, our vehicles were down and out, and my spending account was sitting at zero. Now, growing up, this moment would've felt like another blow that warranted us to kick-start survival mode, but because my wife and I had been playing offense for years, we barely reacted. Let me explain in terms of spiritual/emotional and financial offense.

SPIRITUAL/EMOTIONAL

When I walked in the house and saw the water pouring down, my first reaction was to laugh. I instantly thought about how hilarious it was that we were putting the house on the market in seven days and now it was flooded. Plus, all of my equipment was destroyed. To the average person, that wouldn't be funny at all, but for the past few years, I'd learned to look at tragic situations differently. From a spiritual standpoint, I've learned that when bad things happen or when things get removed from my life, God has something great waiting for me around the corner. So, in my mind, within the first two minutes of being in the house, I began wondering how the situation was going to benefit me in the long run. I knew it was time to find solitude so I could hear from God and uncover the answers. I felt an extreme level of peace, like when my mother passed.

FINANCIAL

We knew we could easily buy another car because we'd been building up our credit. Although my spending account was at zero, I had been following the Richest Man in Babylon and had saved a few grand in my business account. I knew I could borrow from the business account if needed and use the money to make even more money. As far as the flooded house was concerned, we weren't even living there. I had purchased another property at a housing auction a year and a half prior. I'd fixed it up and moved the family in. The flooded home had a mortgage and was insured. The insurance company gave us close to $30,000, which was a blessing. They also reimbursed me for all of my podcast equipment that was damaged. In addition, I was able to apply for federal grants because of COVID, so the whole setback ended up being a blessing.

So if you're someone who wants to break a cycle, know that the cycle will be broken when you play both offense and defense. Hard times will hit everyone, no matter who you are. You could be Warren Buffet or a homeless man. When you play good offense, you have a better chance of taking life's storms on the chin and benefiting from them. But when you continuously play defense, you'll have a harder time dealing with anxiety, depression, and other mental health triggers because there will be no breaks and no victories to build upon.

"You're already struggling. Why not get a reward for it?" — Eric Thomas

This mindset from ET the hip-hop preacher is key. If we all have struggles, why not be someone who deals with them and enjoys the benefits of your hard work? Progression is the key to enjoying life and dealing with its struggles, and the only way to progress is to play offense. Look at the sixteen hours you have to work with in a day and figure out how you can use that time to progress. The first step toward progress and offense is knowing what the mission is and putting together a plan, which we will discuss next.

9

WHAT'S THE PLAN?

When it comes to breaking any negative cycle, I believe it's important to make a plan about what you will achieve or what benefit you want to experience. You must figure out what you want and what your purpose is and give yourself an end result or a finish line. This may sound simple, but it's extremely important. You must be 100 percent clear on what you want and where you want to go. If needed, drop all your distractions and find solitude until you can figure this out. For example, if you want to stop attracting abusive partners, then your finish line might involve finding happiness within yourself and building a relationship that involves healthy communication. If you want to get away from living paycheck to paycheck, your finish line may involve having a source of passive income, running a business, or finding a better-paying job.

In my case, I was tired of financially struggling and not being able to help my mother. I was tired of all my business ventures only achieving average success. I was tired of feeling like I had to sell drugs and live a lie. I was tired of sleeping around with multiple women and feeling emotionally empty. I was tired of feeling like a loser because all of my hard work amounted to absolutely nothing. So, my finish line was to turn my media skills into a billion-dollar company, be in a healthy and powerful relationship, have the discipline to remain faithful, and find my purpose through media.

I have to be honest; it took me some time to figure out what my purpose and finish line was. It was not easy. People who know me may say I've always been living this life, but for a long time, I thought I was supposed to inspire the world through music. It wasn't until I actually asked God to reveal my purpose that he showed me I was supposed to build a media company. The solution was right under my nose, but I had never actually asked or sought it out. So, before you continue reading, take a moment to uncover what your finish line is.

HOW TO FIND YOUR PURPOSE AND FINISH LINE

"If you can't figure out your purpose, figure out your passion, for your passion will lead you right into your purpose."—T. D. Jakes

Purpose is so hard to discuss because you can't possibly know it until you know it. You can't just choose a purpose; it's something that comes out of you. The most important piece of the puzzle is usually the hardest to find or figure out.

Figuring out what your purpose is or having a clear finish line is life-changing. It'll help you feel charged and hungry for success at all moments. You'll have clarity, and you'll find yourself striving for improved focus and development. Understand that your finish line or purpose will only come to you when you're ready for it, so don't rush this process. People tend to ask, "How do I know where I'm supposed to be?" or "How do I make sure I'm ready?" I'm sorry to tell you, but I don't have an answer. All I can say is that you must consciously want to be ready, then you must recognize when you weren't ready in the past and learn from those moments.

Has someone older ever given advice that, at the time, you thought was irrelevant, only for it to hit you years later? If so, you've probably thought about where you'd be or what you'd be doing had you listened the first time. I really want you to think about why you couldn't hear them at that moment. Why weren't you ready to internalize their message? If you can figure out what turned you off about receiving the message at the time, that's great. Maybe it was boredom or maybe you were focused on something else. Once you figure out what kept you from hearing them, keep that feeling in mind to fight that resistance next time. The same thing applies when it comes to your purpose. Years ago, when someone told me something I couldn't fully understand, I would just push through the boredom and wait for them to shut up so I could move on. Now, I take that feeling as a sign that they could be sharing a message that will take me to the next level. So now I politely cut them off and ask them to start over. I've become extremely curious and honest about what I don't understand, and I'm not afraid to pull my phone out and take notes. More often than not, I learn something groundbreaking in these interactions.

Before we discuss more ways to find your purpose or finish line, let's discuss what it can feel like to not know your purpose or not have a finish line in your sights. At certain moments, you may feel a sense of dissatisfaction, a lack of peace, and deep sadness. When your life doesn't match up with who you truly are, things will feel off balance. Do not ignore these feelings. Learn to take these signs as a message that you are missing the mark and need to adjust your daily habits. If you can never seem to feel at peace at your job, then you may not have the same energy and passion for it that you used to, which can cause you to feel upset. This could be a sign that there is more for you and it's time to move on. If the staff at your company is quitting, unhappy, and unmotivated, then maybe your company's strategies need to change. Long story short, if you feel like good things aren't happening or you can't find peace in your current situation, then it's possibly a sign that it's time to make some changes. I can't speak for everyone, but the days I spent outside of my purpose were dark and depressing. Right now, I'm only halfway in my purpose because I'm still working a full-time job. I can still feel the burn anytime I'm not fully focused on the end goal.

Now let's talk about how you can figure out your purpose. First, let me say I don't have a definite answer for this; no one does. I can only give you suggestions based on my personal story. Second, make sure you don't think too deeply into this. Your purpose could be simple, and you could miss it by thinking it's some grand idea, or you could overlook it by comparing yourself to others. I created content, videos, and music for years and never realized that my purpose was to start and run a media company. The only thing required to find your purpose is fully accepting that there is a purpose, fully believing that you will find it, feeling entitled to knowing it, and being ready to make the necessary changes. Ignore that inner voice that wants to compare you to others or think about what others have to say. Just be present and honest without fear. Once you master this, you can avoid being like that teenager who refuses to listen to their elders.

Here are some categories you can explore to find your purpose: your calling, problem-solving, innovation, and service. I encourage you to pause after each section and write down how this category may apply to your life. It's important to not skip over this part because writing out these details will help you organize your thoughts and get some answers.

YOUR CALLING

People often say that your purpose is something God has called you to. In these cases, you'll feel something specific deep in your bones. You may have deep knowledge about this area, or you may be extremely passionate about it. What subject do you obsess over and are willing to stay up all night doing or looking into? I've always been able to stay up for hours working on projects, researching topics, and editing small details that would drive the average person crazy.

Another sign that you've found your calling is if the task comes easy to you. One thing that has always been easy for me is coming up with solutions to challenges. I didn't realize problem-solving had been the heart and soul of all my creations, but assessing problems and seeking solutions has been the driver of my purpose.

Pause here and write down what field or industry you think your calling might be in, like service to others, sports, or nutrition. What field of work drives you the most?

PROBLEM-SOLVING

The second category to explore is problem-solving. Every one of us has a problem we're close to, a problem that can no longer be ignored and that we likely have both passion and solutions for. Maybe you grew up in a poor neighborhood and you think you have a solution. Maybe you're someone who continues to stay in unhealthy, possibly abusive, relationships. You may not know how to change the actions of other people, but you can figure out what it is about you that keeps attracting the same type of person. Whatever your situation is, it's important to spend time figuring out a realistic solution for the problem you're currently facing.

INNOVATION

The third category you should focus on is innovation. You could be someone who creates a niche to take something to another level. Everyone has faced specific situations that have exposed them to different walks of life and have given them different perspectives on the world. Sometimes these experiences can help someone connect dots in a way they wouldn't have been able to if they didn't have a diverse upbringing. Think about the first preacher who collaborated with a musician and gave the people what we now know as praise and worship or gospel music. Think about Steve Jobs, who had a vision to put a computer and telephone together and make it small enough to fit in your pocket. Think about the hip-hop pioneers who combined a disco beat with spoken words.

So, understand that every unique circumstance you've been forced to experience, whether it was positive or negative, has given you an opportunity for innovative discovery. As a child, businessman Robert Kiyosaki's parents were both financially stagnant school teachers, but his friend's father was a growing entrepreneur. This glimpse into another life gave Kiyosaki the drive to eventually write Rich Dad Poor Dad, a personal finance guidebook. Similarly, imagine a woman who grew up in a family that owned real estate and taught her the ins and outs of the business. Later in life, that young woman ends up in a ten-year abusive relationship. When she finally breaks free from that relationship, she decides to start a nonprofit for women to have somewhere to go when they're abused. Combining her real estate knowledge and experience with abuse allowed her to create a women's shelter.

SERVICE

The last category to think about is service. How can you serve others with the gifts, talents, and insights you have? Now, I'm not saying you should put others before you or be a people pleaser, but how can you use your gifts to serve others and add value to their lives?

Many successful entrepreneurs often talk about how people can make money with their innate gifts and talents. This goes back to figuring out what comes easy to you, and I'm definitely not against this strategy. However, I've always been more interested in the brands that have been around forever and have built a powerful reputation. To me, the people and companies that put serving others first make more money in the long run than those who simply chase money. For example, Amazon may look like a company that is after maximum profit, and of course, maximum profit is on its agenda, but its first goal is figuring out how it can best serve its customers. Amazon originally took off because it made online book shopping easier for consumers. It eventually expanded its services to virtually every product on the market. The first question they ask themselves is "How can we make the shopping experience faster and easier for the consumer?" And just to be clear, I am not saying Jeff Bezos, Steve Jobs, or Mark Zuckerberg aren't thinking about how they can make money; I'm simply stating that they also focus on how they can serve others and solve problems.

Take a deeper look into companies that are no longer around, like Verve energy drinks. I remember when this product was the hottest thing smoking, but the company ended up shutting down due to their business practices. According to its nutritional facts, Verve was a healthier energy drink, with less sugar and sodium compared to Monster energy drinks. But because the company's executives chose to invest in their company using a pyramid scheme, they destroyed everything they built. Other examples of fallen companies are Circuit City, Toys "R" Us, Blackberry, and Myspace. The average person will say these companies just failed to innovate, but that statement isn't good enough for me. I believe they couldn't innovate because serving their customers wasn't their first priority. When a company culture is centered around how it can serve others, everyone involved is forced to stay in touch with their humanity. When you focus on money instead, you'll find yourself doing any and everything to get that money, which could land you in a situation you can't bounce back from.

This is something politicians are either good or bad at. A decision made today could either hurt or help a politician six years from now.

WHAT'S THE VISION?

After you get an idea of what your purpose is, it is time to put together your long-term vision. What does your future look like? Think ten years from now, five years from now, and a year from now. Take your time, think big, and ignore doubts. This process can take weeks or even years to figure out, and your goals may change over time. But the key is making time every day to sit in silence and get the answers you need. Your vices, worldly desires, and daily activities will do everything they can to distract you from finding solitude, but being selfish and finding time to do this is extremely important. I'm not saying it's easy, but it's a must.

This is the part of the process where you clearly state

what you want out of life. This is the time to make a clear decision. A lot of people will say they are not happy in their current job, relationship, or life, but if you ask them what they want or what their future vision is, they can't answer. They've never taken the time to sit down and make a clear decision. Pause here and ask yourself, "What do I want?" Be specific. Do you have an answer to that question right now? Most people do not. So take your time and think this through; however avoid overthinking it. This isn't about being perfect, and you definitely shouldn't stress over it. Listen to yourself and find answers in the peace. As you continue to sit in solitude, your vision will become clearer and change for the better.

So, if you haven't already, pause here and start writing out what you want. Ignore the doubts and critical voices from yourself and others. No one has to know what you've written. Just be free and write until you come to a bold conclusion of what you want. Once you've made a firm decision about what you want your future to look like in five to ten years, you can work backward and plan out what needs to be done monthly, weekly, and daily to reach that long-term goal. You not only need to know what tasks need to be done daily, but you also need a process for keeping yourself on track. It is easy to get distracted, so some people create vision boards or physically write out their goals so they are always visible. I use the Notes app on my phone and Google Docs to keep my visions and plans organized. I have one note for my long-term vision and a separate one for my weekly vision. Once a week, I look at the long-term vision and make changes if needed, then I set my goals for the week and write them on the weekly goals page. At the end of the week, I can physically see what goals I accomplished and what still needs to be done. If I ever have a moment during the day where I think, What do I need to get done?, I can look at my weekly/daily goals and knock something else off the list.

10

ACCOUNTABILITY CAN GUARANTEE SUCCESS

"Imagine what a sports team would look like without a coaching staff and a business department. Chaos, right? That's what a life without accountability is like."
—Seth Whitted

I can't express how impactful accountability, or a lack thereof, is. Accountability is another game changer because it's the tool that helps you focus and get things done no matter what happens in life. It's so easy for life's circumstances and our personal vices to provide us with excuses for not achieving our goals, but accountability says, "I don't care. We've got goals to accomplish."

Think back to your school-age days. Most likely one of your parents made sure you were awake for school every morning and held you to a certain standard of being on time and having good attendance. That's a form of accountability. Other forms of accountability for school attendance were the actual attendance policy that resulted in detention, suspension, or sports ineligibility if it was ignored. I know a lot of people reading this book might not have grown up with this type of dynamic, but I urge you to entertain the thought for a moment.

Using this example, what do you think would happen if a particular person or process was holding you accountable to have great attendance for thirteen years and then, boom, you found yourself alone at college or in the job market with no one holding you accountable? The average person would not keep up that attendance standard. According to the Education Data Initiative, 40 percent of freshmen drop out of college. One of the reasons for these dropouts is finances, and another is a lack of preparation and self-discipline.

Imagine if a sports team didn't have a coach, someone to organize workouts and make them mandatory, someone to organize and structure the practices so the team worked together to become better, reach goals, and get a shot at winning the championship. If practice was left to the players, there's a very high chance they would just show up on game day. Every now and then, you'll find a team that has players who step up and organize these things, but those people are far and few between. Without having a process of accountability, you will live your life like a sports team that doesn't have a coaching staff, administrators, or an athletic director. All of the people behind the scenes hold the team accountable in different ways to achieve success.

Because accountability is simply taking responsibility of your habits and knowing the why behind your actions, there are many ways you can implement it in your life. But first, let's understand the difference between internal and external accountability.

INTERNAL ACCOUNTABILITY

Internal accountability is understanding why you're on your mission and using your inner drive to get things done. If you don't execute on your mission, you may feel shame, guilt, or depression. In my opinion, the greatest people to walk this earth are masters of self-accountability. If you study people like Tom Brady, Michael Jordan, Jay-Z, Warren Buffet, or Floyd Mayweather, you'll find they all had an inner drive to stay focused and go the extra mile. It didn't matter if someone around them was telling them to or not; they developed a process that reminded them to not only execute but outwork both themselves and the competition.

You can hold yourself accountable by remembering why you're doing what you're doing. Write it down; put sticky notes everywhere. Set deadlines for yourself. Do anything you can to remind yourself of your goal.

My internal accountability comes during my personal meetings. I take the time to read my yearly goals once a week and ask myself if I'm any closer to achieving them or if I've wasted too much time. I then make adjustments based on this feedback so I can be more effective next week. For example, this week I only accomplished two out of the six goals I set, which made me realize I was spread too thin. I had made too many commitments to other people. Although the commitments were beneficial, they took away from my top priorities. So, I made a decision to not make any more commitments until I have the time. I must complete my goals before I can execute on someone else's. I wrote these changes and goals on my weekly goal list, and before I went to bed that night, I chose the most important goals to knock out the next day. In the morning, I took another look at those daily goals and attacked them like a mad man. The list also comes in handy when I feel like there's nothing for me to do. Looking at my priorities reminds me to stay locked in and execute on what's next.

EXTERNAL ACCOUNTABILITY

Before I break down external accountability, I want to speak with those who are reserved, prideful, or private. I want to warn you now that this is an area where you're going to have to decide if your comfort zone or pride and your issue with letting people close to you is more important than succeeding at your long-term goals. Now, if you're a master of self-accountability and you can consistently execute on your plans, even when no one is looking, then I salute you. But if you know you suck at holding yourself accountable and always cut corners or look for an easier route, then I suggest you move away from your comfort zone.

External accountability involves having a support

system of people who know what your goals are and have the green light to hold you accountable. They're the annoying mentor, brother, sister, cousin, or friend who doesn't care how you feel and pushes you toward your goals no matter what. This is the role I've taken on in my friendships and family dynamics, the Dame Dash type. This is the kind of person no one else can stand, but at the same time, they appreciate them because they push everyone to be better. I know I annoy my family, but I also know they're more likely to execute on their plans if they know they're going to have to see me soon. I'm cool with being that guy. If you're that person in your family, keep applying the pressure and be OK with people being frustrated with you behind your back.

External accountability can also come in the form of results, or lack thereof. Let's say you have a plan to eat healthier, work out, and lose twenty pounds in two months. If a month goes by and you've gained five pounds, then the results are letting you know that those three workouts plus the cheat meals and late-night snacking are to blame. You must stick to the script until you see results. You must sacrifice anything that goes against your goals until you see results. Don't ignore the results, whether they're good or bad. People often say, "But I do work out" or "I don't eat fast food like that anymore," but unless you have some underlying health issue that's keeping you from staying on track, the results don't lie.

Public accountability is another form of external accountability. Say you want to put out content every day on social media. You could do it yourself, or you could tell your friends that you plan on posting every day for the next thirty days and you want them to hold you accountable. For this to work, you must swallow your pride and step out of your comfort zone.

If you don't feel like there's anyone in your life who

could hold you accountable, it could be because you're interested in something other people aren't, everyone around you is pessimistic and you don't trust their viewpoints, or you only want to be held accountable by people who have succeeded in the area you're focused on. This was me. So, I began by following the people I looked up to on social media, like Jay-Z, Eric Thomas, Gary Vanderchuk, Steve Jobs, Marcus Garvey, Muhammad Ali, and a few others. I consumed myself with their content when I was working out or driving. I could literally hear them in my ear throughout the day holding me accountable. Take advantage of social media. Join the appropriate groups, follow experts in your field, and hire a mentor. Unfollow anyone or anything that doesn't encourage growth and accountability.

Next, take advantage of group chats. My bro Myke Wells put together a group chat with at least twelve guys who are entrepreneurs, investors, or interested in investing. We text and talk about investing of all types, and we grow together. I'm in another group chat that's focused on black empowerment, another with folks in the music/media industry, and another one that is funny and inspiring.

The last tip that has been the most helpful for me is to create a personal advisory board. (I noticed that successful individuals, like Jay-Z and Warren Buffet, had advisory boards. In the mental health field, all of the clients have a support team, from payee for finances, nurses, doctors, day-to-day staff, behavioral specialists, and support coordinators who make sure everyone does their job.) Only the wealthy, adults with mental and emotional diagnosis and children with developmental issues have access to support teams that intentionally focus on their personal and professional development. So, I decided to start my own. I took notice of the areas of my life that could use an extra pair of eyes and asked people who were experts in these areas to invest an hour a month to meet with me and the other board members. This group of people helps me make sure my vision and goals are clear, holds me accountable, gives me insight and feedback, exposes my blind spots, and generally assists me with anything they can. There are so many ways you can be held accountable. Do not overlook this step because accountability can and will push you ahead faster.

EXECUTION

The last step is simple and plain. Every day, focus on executing on your important goals. Avoid being distracted by the small tasks that get you nowhere. My wife and I argue all the time because I sometimes leave the house a little messy or take a while to put my laundry away. To her, I'm sloppy, but for me, that thirty minutes spent folding is a waste of time. I'd rather sacrifice folded laundry and use that time for an important task that will generate me enough money so I can eventually hire someone to fold my laundry!

I understand why she is willing to spend her time cleaning because it is therapeutic and her moment of solitude, but it does the opposite for me. I hate it, and when I do clean, I often rush to finish as fast as possible and get back to doing something that is relevant to my mission. To me, I'm just going to end up washing these clothes again and eventually throwing them away. There's no long-term gain in folding them; it can wait.

11

SHOWING RESULTS IS THE BEST WAY TO INSPIRE OTHERS

"When I get rich, we all get rich. No more licks; we out the bricks, and that's it." —Seth Whitted "Rough Draft"

If you come from a low-income, high-crime area, most likely the people in your community are going through similar hardships. People are close-knit, and in my opinion, these collective struggles bring the community closer together, causing your neighbors to want to see you win. Yes, there are selfish people who don't want someone else to get ahead, especially before them, but it's easy to recognize them. Th e majority of the people you know are in tough situations like yourself, and they want more too. I've always been family-

and community-oriented, and I always wanted others to do better. If I learned something valuable, I wanted others to learn it as well. If there was money to be had, I was the guy who made sure everyone knew about it so they could take advantage. Taking care of everyone around me has always been a dream of mine. I used to always say in my music, "When I get rich, we all get rich." I meant that then, and I still do today.

Would you believe me if I told you this giving trait of mine has caused problems for me? For one, it distracts me. It also causes me to feel a lot of guilt and shame, and it has even caused me to unconsciously self-sabotage. This giving trait is actually people-pleasing disguised as being a good man who cares about everyone. It runs so deep for me that I take it as my personal responsibility to make sure my friends, loved ones, and community grow with me. It wasn't until recently that I figured this out about myself. My wife had been trying to show me this blind spot for years, and I just thought she couldn't understand because she wasn't the giving type. The only reason I was able to see this people-pleasing trait for myself was because I followed my rule and principle of exploring all the criticism my loved ones give me. This is why it's important to actually commit to the rules and principles we set in chapter 1.

In my personal experience, the process of growth and success is as follows: 1) Set a goal or recognize a problem. 2) Find knowledge that either helps you reach the goal or shows you how to fix the problem. 3) Apply that knowledge and consistently execute the plan. This has always been my biggest issue. The key word is consistently because I always put projects out, met deadlines, and accomplished goals, but the moment I started to outgrow others or gain some momentum that would separate me from those around me, my people-pleasing voice would remind me that I needed to bring them along. So, I would shift my focus to presenting the information to family, friends, and coworkers and making sure I was getting the message through. But the opposite happened. I normally managed to get two out of ten people to understand me, but the other eight would dismiss the information, argue that they don't believe in it, or be halfway invested. They weren't disrespectful; they just didn't have the passion for the information like I did.

Attempting to convince them became an unhealthy obsession of mine. When we went our separate ways for the day, I would still think about how I could convince them. I could be driving, lying in bed, or pacing around the house, debating with them in my mind. Why can't you see this? I started vlogging the information like a motivational speaker, hoping they would listen. It took over the music I was making. I would seize every opportunity to teach what I had learned. It was an addiction I had a hard time breaking.

"People don't do what you tell them to do; they become who you are." —Eric Thomas

One day, my wife said, "You're always trying to help people and all they do is waste your time. Look at how much time you've spent helping this person only for them to not do anything with what you told them." She was right. I was busy trying to fix people who never asked for my help. I started exploring this idea by simply Googling "Why do I try to help everyone?". Months of looking into this and learning about people-pleasing behavior reminded me of the time I spoke at a local high school.

Every three months, Miss Tammy Collier invited a group of alumni men to come back and speak with the young men in school. When I spoke, I remember some of the kids listening, some dozing off, and others not fully engaged. But when my bro Marco Harris started speaking, everyone was immediately engaged and attentive. At that moment, I realized one of the many solutions to my problem. Marco had grown to be one of the few successful entrepreneurs on this side of Pennsylvania. When the kids saw him, they saw his nice cars, barbershop, and fresh outfit. These things might not be exactly what they want, but they act as bright, flashy signs that say, "This man knows what he's talking about." Although I shared some great information to motivate them, I didn't have the success to visually show them why they should listen. That moment reassured me that step three—consistently executing your plan—was the key. From that moment on, I focused my attention strictly on that. I waited on others to ask for advice instead of giving it freely, and I made sure people earned my time and information. I have to admit, this battle was not simple. If you feel you have an issue with people-pleasing or saying no, I understand and I suggest you read Not Nice by Dr. Aziz Gazipura.

"You know how to kill a big dream? Tell it to a small-minded person. God gave you a big idea that you believe is brilliant, but you told it to your friends and family members and they shot it down. They can't see the brilliance in it because it wasn't shown to them." —Steve Harvey

If you battle this people-pleasing habit or feel guilty for outgrowing your family and friends, but you want to grow and help others at the same time, I understand. I felt the same way. Here is a list of rules I made for myself to accomplish this goal.

1. Always put yourself, your purpose, and your goals

first. Establish what you need and must do to grow before you do anything else. I'm a lot better at telling people no these days. I've learned that my goals and plans are more important for my career than theirs. I've freed myself of feeling like I need to drop everything I'm doing to help someone build something they want.

2. Only give to others what they earn and deserve. I realized that the reason people took my help for granted was because they often don't appreciate things they don't work for. So, if someone asks me how to invest in stocks, I no longer give a full rundown. I tell them what apps I use and some beginner steps for research, then I tell them to hit me up if they have any more questions. Eighty percent of the time, I never hear from them again. But I give more information to that other 20 percent to the

point where we're bouncing information off each other and they become a strong ally. This has saved me so much time and energy. I'm not as bitter toward the 80 percent as I used to be. If others aren't ready for the information, then they're just not ready.

3. It is not your responsibility to make others ready to receive valuable information. If you tell someone something they can't understand, there's no point in arguing. Just take it as a sign that they're not in the place to hear the information yet. Understand that this will hurt and that you will possibly lose people you thought were going to be around for life.
4. Understand that there are givers and takers, and some people live to take. They may not realize they're a taker, but when you make sure you're taking care of yourself, you will disrupt their process and

they may take it personally. This is a good time to clear your space of people who aren't good for you.

5. Less convincing and more consulting. If you have valuable information to share that others want to know, make them pay for it. After all, your time is money.

In 2019, I began my real estate journey by researching real estate's power to take me to the next level financially. I learned obsessively for months, preparing for a housing auction that was coming up. A few like-minded friends and colleagues had already succeeded at this process, so I swallowed my pride and consulted with them in the areas I was unsure about. And as I learned more myself, I shared information with them.

Normally when I'm deeply immersed in a new subject, I call everyone I know to tell them about the new venture, but that time, I stuck to my rules. I reached out to close friends or anyone else I spoke to about growth and told them about the auction. I left the door open by saying, "If you're interested, let me know and I can help." I kept my focus on my own growth. Knowing I would succeed at something that others would potentially miss out on really burned me inside. But I kept going. I reminded myself that I gave everyone the same information I originally received. I even shared tips that took me two years to compile. If they wanted to learn more, they'd have to figure it out themselves, and if they didn't, that was their problem. You have no idea how hard it was for me to not try to convince people to take advantage of the opportunity. But I stuck to the rule.

When the auction came around, I remained focused and locked in. I showed up at the auction with my list of properties, and I bid until I won. I looked around the room to find that the people I had been consulting with were happy to see me secure the property. It felt bittersweet. On one hand, I had just taken a huge step for my family, and I smelled blood in the water because I realized I could do anything if I locked in like that every time. But on the other hand, I felt like I had left people behind. This step in the right direction made me feel guilty inside, and I felt like there was no one to celebrate with. I know it sounds ridiculous, but this is a thought process that haunts many people who feel responsible for others.

I now know that all of these feelings are traits of deep people-pleasing, and they aren't valid. I'm not leaving anyone behind; I'm actually helping more by leading by example. In fact, some of my family members asked me to discuss the housing auction after seeing my success, so we set up a Zoom call and I broke down how I planned for it. Four of the six family members on the Zoom call came to the next auction, and two of them purchased property.

All my life, I thought I had to force information on people, convince them to act on their dreams, and use all my energy to get them to move forward, but I don't think that strategy ever worked. The moment I decided to focus on myself and execute on my goals, people began to ask me questions about how they can succeed too. They actually listened and executed on their plans. This is a prime example of the power of recognizing and removing a blind spot and focusing on yourself and your goals before helping others. The best way to help someone change is to change yourself first.

12

CONCLUSION: BUSINESS MEETING

I hope that after reading this book you can come away from it with a fail-proof process to break your negative cycles and achieve your goals. If you decide to adopt only a few things from this book, make personal business meetings one of them.

Think about every team or organization you've ever been a part of, whether it was at school, in sports, or part of your job. No matter what it was, I guarantee there was always some type of consistent meeting involved. If a team or organization doesn't have meetings, I can guarantee that it is not as organized, focused, or successful as it could be. Meetings are a way for a group of people to set collective goals for success and hold each other accountable.

This is something I picked up from my mother's side of the family. Although my family is big, we remain close by having prayer meetings. My mother used to call me and my siblings into her bedroom for these meetings so we could share what was going on in our lives and how we were going to handle it, then we would pray. I also learned about the importance of meetings from sports and jobs. When I played football, we had meetings after every game to discuss what we could do better. We would watch films on our next opponent and discuss our strategy. At my jobs, we had regular meetings to discuss our progress and creative ways we could do better.

One day, I decided I would have a business meeting with myself, about myself. It started out with me trying to find my purpose, but it has since turned into a weekly meeting that keeps me focused on my current goals. I chose

Saturday and Sunday as the designated days to have these meetings. The meetings are broken down into six sections: faith, health and fitness, family, creativity, Whitted Media, and wealth/investments. When I first started, I had way too many categories, and I realized that nothing was getting accomplished because I was spread way too thin. I decided that, in order to be productive, I would need to focus on just a few things. I decided that these five categories were what I valued the most, and I cut everything else.

Before I begin my meeting, I read or listen to some of the books on my reading list. The books I choose are based on the skills I'm trying to develop or learn. For example, I'm currently reading Getting to Yes by Roger Fisher and William Ury to develop my negotiation skills; Your Next Five Moves by Greg Dinkin and Patrick Bet-David to develop more leadership skills; Black and White by Richard Williams, father of Venus and Serena, for some parenting and marriage tips; the Bible; Not Nice by Aziz Gazipura to get to the root of my people-pleasing addiction; and Power to Heal to increase my faith and use it the way Jesus did. Reading is a critical part of my self-improvement journey because it helps me add to my long-term goals and adjust how I approach my short-term goals. After reading, I can make adjustments to my long-term goals if needed, and then I begin my meeting. I have two notepads on my phone and computer. One is titled "Long-term Goals," and the other is "Short-term Goals." At the top of each notepad is the mission statement for my life. Yes, I wrote a mission statement for my life. My mission statement is written in future tense because I believe that envisioning the destination is key in actually reaching it. My mission statement reads:

"I AM a man of God who influences billions of people at all

times. I protect, provide, and lead my family to true happiness and will show them how to find it. I use media and entertainment to teach God's principles. I have the most consistent multimedia empire, which profits billions. The company helps artists and other companies get exposure to the entire world. I am the most successful artist of all time. When I die, my legacy will inspire thousands of generations."

After I read the mission statement, I go through each category. I cross-check both my long- and short-term goals and remove everything I accomplished that week. Next, I look at my long-term goals and decide what's most important for me to accomplish the next week so I can get closer to that goal. I write this on the short-term goals list. Here's what I came up with at my last meeting:

1. Faith
    a. Long-term goal: God said I will have the

faith to move mountains, prosper, and heal the sick.

   b. Short-term goal: Read or listen to something about faith every day.

2. Health and Fitness
   a. Long-term goals: Be in shape and healthy for the family. Get rid of leaky gut.
   b. Short-term goals: No bread or French fries for the next month. Can only drink alcohol during special occasions. Work out at least four days this week. Only eat animals every other day. Follow the leaky gut diet except on special occasions.
3. Family
   a. Long-term goals: Raise children that work for everything they want. Make sure your wife feels special. Find that dream home.

   b. Short-term goals: Read about the fathers of successful people. Finish Richard Williams's book. Do one special thing this week for your wife. Sit down with your wife and put together a clear vision of what you both want in a dream home.

4. Creativity
   a. Long-term goal: Write a New York Times best-selling book.
   b. Short-term goals: Finish writing chapter 12 of the book, organize the table of contents, and come up with the official title.
5. Whitted Media
   a. Long-term goal: Get the business fully operational so I can work full-time.
   b. Short-term goals: Hire an ad manager who can find sponsors/ads. Develop another

    segment. Meet with social media manager once a week. Hire a grant writer to find grants for business operations.

6. Wealth/Investments
    a. Long-term goals: Find commercial property. Understand NFTs.
    b. Short-term goals: Ask realtors about commercial properties. Find an hour one day this week to look for properties. Take twenty minutes to look up information about NFTs.

The point of the weekly meeting is to organize my priorities so I can enjoy my family, grow as a man and a father, get my health and fitness together, enjoy my hobbies, and try to achieve my long-term goals as soon as I can.

Basically, my goal is to create balance in my life that is centered around my purpose.

"Success is the sum of small efforts repeated day in and day out."

—Robert Collier

Your meeting doesn't have to be the same as mine, but it's important to have some form of a meeting with yourself so you can stay focused and get closer to your goals without wasting time. Each week, adjust the topic of your meeting to best fit your life. This process will not only help you break your negative cycles, but it will also encourage you to take things to another level. This takes discipline and dedication. It is not easy, but it is a must.

Pause once more and come up with a meeting schedule for yourself. It may be difficult to dedicate yourself to this at first, but once you get in the groove, it will run smoothly. After you decide on the day, make a few categories you would like to cover. Start with what you value the most, and try not to list too many things at once.

If you've made it to the end of this book, you're someone who's hungry and eager to change your life. With this book, I hope to inspire others to get out of their own way and write their own stories. We all have gifts and the ability to find our purpose. We also all have vices and internal battles that prevent us from reaching our full potential.

This book is here to remind you that your success and desires do not care about your circumstances. No matter what you're going through or how you feel, life is going to keep moving. I challenge you to look at the negative circumstances you experience as obstacles you will overcome instead of reasons you should quit. It is key to figure out what is holding you back and come up with a plan that can protect you. Become obsessed with figuring out the most efficient and effective way to reach your goals and break the negative cycles in your life, and you will find the contentment you seek.

References

1. Economy, Peter. "This Is the Way You Need to Write Down Your Goals for Faster Success," Inc., [date accessed]. https://www.inc.com/peter-economy/this-is-way-you-need-to-write-down-your-goals-for-faster-success.html.

2. Martin, Sharon. "Using Your Strengths to Get Happier," PsychCentral, February 12, 2016. https://psychcentral.com/blog/imperfect/2016/02/using-your-strengths-to-get-happier.

3. McQuaid, Michelle. "Ten Reasons to Focus on Your Strengths," Psychology Today, November 11, 2014. https://www.psychologytoday.com/us/blog/functioning-flourishing/201411/ten-reasons-focus-your-strengths.

Made in USA - Kendallville, IN
50463_9798987299005
07.29.2024 1947